Talking To My Self

Evolving on Purpose

Tanis T McRae

Cover design: "Visionary Healer – She Who Walks Through Doors" Wendybyrd Smith, Pastels on Paper. Sedonasoulseer.com

Author Photo: Tryna Gower

Tanis McRae
c/o The Healing I
Contact information can be found at - thehealingi.com

The intent of this intuitive teacher and author is for information and education purposes only. Any medical conditions discussed or referred to specifically or implied should be cared for under the direction of a physician. Proper care from a physician should not be avoided, delayed or disregarded when there is reason to consult a physician.

It is the intent of this author and intuitive teacher to assist you in your quest for optimal health, wellness and evolvement. There is no intention to diagnose or prescribe any physical or emotional disease in any way.

ISBN: 978-1-62747-129-9
Ebook ISBN: 978-1-62747-130-5

Dedication

To my family both genetic and spiritual,
And to my boys Dave, Niklas and Aidan.
You are the reason I know love.

To my Dad and my spiritual sidekick Zoe,
I think of you every day.

Contents

Chapter 1
A White Picket Fence

"Celebrations rarely surround choices to follow personal truth. In fact, quite the contrary. Not only may others fail to celebrate, they may actually subject you to ridicule. What? You're thinking for yourself? You're deciding on your own? You're applying your own yardsticks, your own judgments? Your own values? Who do you think you are anyway? And indeed that is precisely the question you are answering. Why even start off on such a path? Where is the incentive? What is the reason? The reason is ridiculously simple. THERE IS NOTHING ELSE TO DO."

> ~ Neale Donald Walsch,
> *Conversations With God, Book 1*

You know that old joke; what are the two certain things in Life? Death and Taxes...well you can add 'catalyst' to the list. A catalyst, when used to your advantage is like a slingshot taking you from one position to another very quickly.

When you are being catalyzed it can feel like pain, suffering, misery, major changes, accidents and chaos. Sound familiar? The statement often accompanies them: "Why is this happening? Or "Oh no, not again!" One thing is for certain, they are happening in your life all the time. When you recognize and work with them, they can become very powerful creation tools.

Catalysts can be a negative or a positive experience but they always create movement, all ways.

Like every other human being on Earth I have experienced many moments in my life that catalyzed me into going a new direction or shook up my beliefs so much I had to change my mind and subsequently the belief.

I must be truthful and tell you that I don't have a tremendously tragic tale, a near death experience or even a health crisis that will draw you into my story and marvel at my miraculous recovery or experience.

I, in fact, live the quintessential 'white picket fence' kind of life.

I am happy and content and I am not tortured by a secret yearning for anything else; yet somewhere deep down I have always felt called to expand in some way, to be more than the sum of my parts and to make a positive difference in the world I live in.

I know there are many other books and information out there but I believe my insights and the process of healing I have learned along the way is worth sharing. That in telling you how I have helped my Self and others you will find synchronicities and relatable information that will assist you in your life experience.

Isn't that why we read something in the first place? Because we resonate with it we relate to it because we have had a similar experience or a voyeuristic need to see how someone else is moving through their experience. We can compare and evaluate where we are in our journey and get some relative insight into our own progress.

I know that my white picket fence existence can be just as intriguing and as relatable as any other story out there. I feel like I have done something wonderful and amazing. I have consciously and deliberately chosen to evolve and grow my Self not just in reaction to a major event but with an honest and earnest intention to become the best version of my Self I can be. To tackle the inner realities I have created and break them down to their individual ingredients and examine every bit of who I am.

I dedicated my Self to healing and discovering who I am and in that decision I was determined that no part of me would go unexamined. I journeyed into parts of myself and then decided, **consciously decided,** if that was an aspect I would keep, or if I would seek to transform it. I constantly asked my Self these questions:

Who am I Spiritually, Emotionally, Mentally, and Physically? Who am I really? Who do I want to be?

I would be brutally honest and constantly challenge my Self to look in the mirror and decide who I am every chance I get. This self-realization process is not for the faint of heart, you will NEVER be able to point a finger outward ever again because you will be doing a lot of internal work here. That willingness to examine the Self and stop blaming things and people on the outside for who you are will be what will move you forward like nothing else because healing is always an inside job.

I see healing and evolving as similar processes. As we let go of, or transform, the things inside of us that cause us pain, fear or trauma we evolve past those limitations and improve upon what has happened to us. Through this process of letting go we begin to create a new and different understanding of who we are in our life experience.

Evolving is moving from a simple form to a more complex form and the traits that are used to evolve something are the ones that ensure survival and strength. The act of healing is to become more sound or healthy. These have become interchangeable terms to me and I will use them in that way throughout the book because I want you to know that as you choose to heal you automatically choose to evolve as well.

I have always known on every level that I am not satisfied with just maintaining the status quo and that I was not content to stop learning or evolving. I don't want to just float through life and not contribute to it in any way. It is one of the reasons I was called to become a schoolteacher. It felt like I was working for the greater good, and affecting the world in a positive way.

I felt a calling to the process of healing as strongly as I felt about teaching, and I soon realized this was the direction I wanted to take – so I quit teaching. Yikes!

I left a secure career and embarked on learning as much as I could about something very few people believed in and many were sceptical and even fearful of the direction I was taking. I met with resistance from many of my friends and acquaintances.

I found out that to achieve that expansion I would need to change who I am at a very intimate level, not set out to change the world but rather to start at home base, to fundamentally change whom I am.

As I explored the teachings of various authors and spiritual leaders, I made it my mission to absorb and exemplify the teachings they shared; to bring these philosophies into my day-to-day process and become the concepts they were sharing so generously.

I started to EVOLVE ON PURPOSE.

Which brings me back to the catalyst because this human journey of mine did not occur without those all important catalysts; one of those amazing defining moments when you are balanced on the brink of change and then you get to decide to step forward or go back into your comfort zone and wait until the next leap of faith presents itself.

Well my precipice of change happened when my Mom had reached the critical point of illness. For a great deal of my life, my Mom was not well. She was not sick per se she just didn't thrive. For forty years they poked, prodded, tested, diagnosed and scratched their proverbial heads in confusion, as nothing seemed to be the definitive answer to what she was experiencing.

She developed many sensitivities: to food, fabric, and smells. She had eliminated all but twelve foods in her diet, no dairy, no gluten, no preservatives, only unadulterated food was ok. It was fortunate that we lived on our own family farm, so all her vegetables, meat and fruit (berries etc.) were home grown, and this eliminated the unknown factor of how her food was produced and what ingredients it contained.

Her allergies to fabric were the most restrictive. She could not have any synthetic material on her person at all. This meant no nylon, no polyester, no acrylic; only natural fibres like cotton, wool and silk did not cause her to break out in hives.

Imagine buying your underwear and the first thing you have to do is rip out all the seams because of the polyester thread and replace them all with cotton thread. Imagine not being able to wear your seatbelt without a leather covering, or walk on your carpet, or sit in an upholstered chair or hug your friend who is wearing clothes that hurt you, sleep on a mattress or go to a gathering where everyone is wearing some sort of fragrance.

Now before you get all new age organic on me and tell me about the organic movement, I want to remind you that we are circa 1970-2000 here. Organic material and food was NOT in your local supermarket and not really considered at all by the mainstream population. Couple that with location (we live in a remote part of Canada) limited financial means, now you may have a picture of how restrictive and isolating her experience was.

We all did what we could to eliminate the discomfort. We bought cotton clothes for our kids so they could hug Grandma, we put plastic sheets on mattresses, eliminated all artificial scents from our homes, and made sure we had furniture she could sit on. She wore shoes on the carpet and brought her own food everywhere she went and travelled in their motor home so she could get out and visit the people she loved and still have some control over the environment to a certain extent.

For many, many years she lived this restricted life and she never allowed her limitations to depress her. She soldiered on changing and accommodating as best she could and still live a normal life. But after so many years, we started to see that it was taking its toll and that she was starting to give up – her giant indomitable will was wearing out and she started to isolate herself and not go places. Then her doctor said; "I just don't think we are going to be able to help you." This seemed to leech all the hope she carried. We, her family, were NOT ok with this; we could not let her give up without another fight. I know she had fought long and hard but we just couldn't let her go without trying everything possible.

By 2004 we had access to more alternative health choices than we had in the years previous. I saw that there was a new Naturopath in town and so I called her and we spoke about what my Mom was experiencing.

As a Naturopathic/Holistic Doctor, she believes that we create illness on an energetic, emotional, and physical level and that by using kinaesthetic muscle testing the body will show you where your illness originates. She conducted her assessment in moments then she looked into my Mom's eyes and said, "You have parasites and they are slowly killing their host, we will treat that and boost your immune system, you will be fine." My mom said she almost fell to her knees in gratitude she was so sure she was going to hear much more dire news.

Within just a few months of diet changes and immune boosting remedies, my seventy five year old Mom was so completely on the road to perfect health she booked a bus trip with a friend to Reno!!!!

Many of the food and fabric sensitivities started to dissipate and her physical body became strong again. She fought back those intruders with the same perseverance and care that she did when she accommodated those years of restrictions, and soon we were watching her eat her first unrestricted Thanksgiving meal.

There was one deterrent to her wellness. After forty years of living in restriction she was finding it difficult to remember how to live like a healthy person, one who is not constantly vigilant and hyper-aware of the things you are eating, wearing and exposing yourself to. It had become a pattern to restrict herself.

Our amazing Naturopath, Tamsyn Freeman, who is now an honorary family member and we love her to pieces, explained that your physical health is connected deeply to your emotional well-being and that some of the reasons why Mom was struggling were more emotional that physical in nature.

When I realized that any physical symptoms we experience have emotional components that come from the traumas and emotional events we have had, and that when we do not allow ourselves to heal from them we can create illness, I was astounded and intrigued. We had experienced real time with Mom that when we identified these emotional aspects and consciously changed the thoughts and beliefs around them, that the effect that the experience or event created as a physical symptom or manifestation could actually disappear.

You could heal your Self!

Well needless to say I was insatiable; I started reading anything I could get my hands on and taking courses in all sorts of holistic healing systems. I filled my tool belt with modalities such as Reiki, Quantum Touch, Reconnective Healing, repatterning beliefs, Spiritual Psychology, intuitive counselling and many more.

I discovered some really amazing teachers and mentors along the way: Steve and Barbara Rother of Lightworker.com,

Colette Baron Reid, Don Miguel Ruiz, Debra Silverman, Carissa Schumacher to name a few. But the two most influential teachers I feel have had the most impact on my evolution are, Louise Hay, author of "You Can Heal Your Life", and Neale Donald Walsch, author of "Conversations With God". The information and philosophies they shared inspired much of my Self-healing and beliefs.

As we were exposed to these concepts, philosophies and teachings, my family noticed that the results were significant and immediate. Not only was Mom healing rapidly, we were as well.

As I implemented all these teachings into my day-to-day existence, I found that I really wanted to share what I had learned and experienced so I created a healing business and began to assist others with the same tools I had used for my Self.

The truth is you can take me out of the classroom but you cannot take the teacher out of me. I love to teach. I love a steep learning curve and I love to share everything I have learned. Being called to assist others in their journey was a natural step and soon I was doing personal sessions and teaching workshops on how to heal your Self.

I find that I bring a teacher mentality to healing. The fundamental purpose of teaching is to create independence and self motivated learners. I did not spend twenty years reading to my Grade Ones, I taught them **how** to read so that they became independent and could direct their own learning.

I fundamentally believe that you need to heal your Self, to be responsible for your own healing, and not become dependent on an outside healing facilitator or process no matter how amazing they are.

In fact, I do not want you to just read this book. I want you to have the experience of it.

Engage with it. Use it as a tool because it is meant to be your catalyst and a journey of healing and evolving...just for you!

This book is not a recitation of my journey but rather a compilation of the things I have learned that have helped me and others along the way, and is meant be a practical guide, a self propelled workshop. It includes a plethora of healing tools and directions on how to heal in a practical way.

And you WILL heal.

You are always the person healing your Self. You can have a session with a healing facilitator but YOU will be doing the healing, as it is your experience, beliefs, and your processes that are adjusted. The facilitator is really truly there to hold the space and vibration for you to change. A space for you to feel safe protected and encouraged. This is what I intend for this book to do; create a space and a vibration that you can use to heal your Self.

So if you are going to work your way though this book and heal your Self, we better first talk about vibrators.

Chapter 2
Yup – You're a Vibrator

"If you want to find the secrets of the universe, Think in terms of energy, frequency, and vibration."
~ *Nikola Tesla*

I am going to need you to bear with me for the beginning of this chapter, as it will be somewhat tedious and feel like you are back in school listening to the teacher drone on and on; but if you can manage it this information is the cornerstone of all healing. The basic understanding of energy and what it is and how it works is a vital part of the process, dare I say the most important part of the process. You must be able to discern between dense energy and light energy or none of this stuff will make any sense.

You are basically just energy. The air you breathe is energy, the chair you sit on is energy, everything that IS, is energy and it all comes down to the kind of energy it is. Is it fast or slow? Heavy or light? The healing process is about transforming heavy dense energy into lighter, higher vibrating energy, and it builds on itself just like any process. When you are in Grade One you cannot do Grade Twelve school work. You are not stupid or less than, you are simply at the beginning of your understanding and healing is the same. You get to move through the process of healing you

Self, starting at the beginning and building on your knowledge from there. People are not better healers or better at healing than you they are just further along in the process than you and so are now excellent resources; just as you will be for people who are in 'Grade One' when you are in 'Grade Three.'

And it all begins with a solid understanding of energy.

All things are made up of matter. Matter is anything that has mass and takes up space. It exists in three major states: solid, liquid and gas. What state the matter is in depends on how fast or slow the atoms are vibrating and how much space there is between the atoms.

Even in solids, there is space between the atoms. How tight the atoms are packed determines the density of matter.

Liquids do not hold their shape because there is space between the atoms of a liquid and they are moving slightly all of the time. This allows you to stick your finger into water and pull it back out, letting the water fill back in where your finger once was, because of this aspect all liquids require a container.

Gases not only do not hold their shape they won't even stay put. Gases are always moving. There is so much space between the atoms in gas that you can move around in them easily. Gases will fill up the space and are not as influenced by gravity as a liquid or a solid would be.

Paraphrased from information at:
http://www.chem4kids.com

The conclusion of this mini science lesson is:

Everything vibrates and takes
up space as different densities.

So what in the world does this have to do with healing? Aspects of you exist in all the states of matter right now because parts of you are experiencing being a solid, a liquid and a gas.

We can apply this concept to the experiences and beliefs you are holding right now as well. All the life experiences you have had have a vibration, frequency and density and take up a certain amount of space. The state of that experience will show up in your energy field and in your physical body as either lightness or density depending on how much physical, emotional, spiritual and mental space it 'takes' up.

Experiences that included feelings of anger, abandonment, resentment, hate, fear, etc. produce density and symptoms such as illness, disease, depression etc. These can take up a lot of 'space'.

Experiences based in joy, happiness and love show up as light and weightless in your energy field, and are experienced as contentment, peace, happiness, optimism and motivation. These can feel like they take up less 'space'.

It is also true that:

Matter can move from one state to another, and still be the same substance. Energy has the ability to move matter.

Matter contains energy and energy makes its presence felt through matter.

The state of matter changes when you add more energy.
Paraphrased from information at:
http://www.chem4kids.com

This means you can change your state.

If matter can move from one state to another then that means that you can consciously change the density of the events and experiences you have stored in your energy field and your body, which will then change your vibration and how it affects you. This is how energy helps you to heal.

All forms of matter are composed of energy so that means that when we get past the specific states of matter and how slow or fast the atoms are moving we are energy, pure energy moving at different speeds and frequencies, so the truth is you are pure energy, always have been, and always will be.

If we operate from the truth that you are made up of energy then I would like to address that part of you. I refer to this part of you as your energy field or life-force energy.

If you have ever seen a live bird and a dead bird you will be instantly able to tell which bird has life-force energy present because well... it is alive. This is what I refer to as your energy field or life-force energy as it is the part of you that animates and gives motion to the densest part of you called your body.

How I perceive the life-force energy would be similar to the 'Plasma' state.

Plasma is the fourth state of matter and the most common form of matter in the universe. Plasma in the stars and in the tenuous space between them makes up over 99% of the visible universe. Ordinary solids, liquids, and gases are both electrically neutral and too cool or dense to be in a plasma state.

Plasma consists of a collection of free moving electrons and ions - atoms that have lost electrons. Plasma can be accelerated and steered by electric and magnetic fields, which allows it to be controlled and applied.
http://www.plasmas.org/what-are-plasmas.htm

This would be the most accurate way for me to define "life-force energy". I see the body inside and surrounded by the life-force energy. It is like a vehicle you get in at the beginning of this life and drive for the remainder of that life. I am absolutely certain I asked my energy source for a Ferrari but I got a Fiat.... sigh.

You get to drive the vehicle in this lifetime until your life-force or Soul decides to park it then the life-force leaves that density behind and continues in the plasma state, which I refer to as Universal Energy.

My favourite way to visualize and make sense of the issues that are stored in energy fields around someone is to see it like a giant pool of water filled with different sizes of ice cubes.

The pool of water represents the life-force energy and the ice cubes represent the dense and unresolved issues in our field from experiences we have had.

When we decide to affect these 'ice cubes' we will need to change their vibration or state; so I see the application of energy healing or manipulation of the plasma field then acts like steam from a tea kettle via both the facilitator's vibration and the change of the vibration of the person holding the ice cube in their field.

As they apply the higher faster 'steam' energy called compassion, understanding, perspective and forgiveness to the ice cubes, this affects their density as a solid state by returning them to a liquid which we know has more fluidity and flow so now that experience cannot have the same effect on the energy of that physical body because it's state has been altered.

The reason I love this analogy is because the substance, water, doesn't change. The only thing that is changed is the state, from a solid to a liquid via the application of the highest vibrating state – the steam. You are not dealing with an outside foreign object or energy you are affecting water with water, which is how I see healing – affecting dense energy with light energy.

In basic terms, I do not believe that your life-force energy is all squished up and contained inside your body. I believe that the body is the densest part of the energy field; the life-force energy animates and drives your vehicle and this energy goes on and on forever with no beginning or end. This means that there are no real energy barriers to what you can perceive or access; that you are not finite you are infinite energy but are seemingly having a finite experience.

Imagine if you operated from the knowledge that who you really are is NOT just your body or current reality. Imagine if you believed and lived as if you are really your life-force energy having an experience IN your body, because without the vehicle the life-force energy has nothing to experience life from.

From a pure energy point of view you are everything; all states of matter all the time and you experience yourself as all of it and there is nothing that you are not.

How in the world do you have a separate experience from what you are when you are all of it? You will have to create an illusion of changing states and become denser and separate from that Universal Energy state, and from that seemingly separate state you can experience life.

If we use this concept for our reality then what we can conclude is that the life-force energy creates a temporary container to experience relativity, a finite expression of the infinite if you will. It separates itself from its Self so it can have an experience of its Self and voila! Our tangible existence is created and now we can 'get a life'.

Imagine if you decided to consciously tap into and live from this limitless energy of who you really are. Imagine that you operated from this point of view rather than the limited boundaries of your physical body and mind. This is an amazing concept and an even better reality. This means that you are always aware that your energy field is in contact with everything else's energy field and so there is absolutely no empty space anywhere at any time...and that you are not really separate from anyone or anything.

Add that to the fact that energy cannot be destroyed it can only change form, and only then can we begin to understand that there really is no beginning or end to your energy or life-force it only changes form.

This is how I perceive what people refer to as a 'past life'. It is when the energy of another tangible experience appears in the energy form we have now.

In my experience the reason a past life remembrance or energy occurs in this life-time is because there is a resonance or parallel to a similar life event in this experience right now and the 'ice-cubes' are still there waiting to be healed and have a higher, faster vibration applied to them.

Energy attracts like energy and since you have experienced this before it will show up when you experience it again, regardless of when it happened in your energy field. Remember that the past and future are relative terms and do not apply to the reality of our 'all that is, all the time' universal state which exists as an Absolute reality called "NOW".

Sometimes a real life situation can illustrate much more clearly what I mean than a lengthy explanation:

I was once working with a young man aged eleven who came into this life experience with the condition called asthma. As I read the energy signature of this condition, I realized that the asthma was actually rooted in a past life as a man in World War I who had been exposed to mustard gas. The man felt resentful and angry about his condition and did not make peace with it before he 'died'. This little boy was resonating with the energy of those same resentments and restrictions because he could not have pets, go horseback riding or experience all the things his contemporaries were able to enjoy.

I wondered how could I explain past life energy in a simple straight forward enough way so he could understand it and move this density in his energy field when he isn't even aware of how the root cause could exist outside his known reality.

One of my favourite things about being connected and aware of the limitlessness of my energy field is that I continually ask the Universal Energy questions and because I am tapping into that expanded view and energy I ALWAYS get an answer.

So naturally, I decided to talk about pinecones. I mean it's obvious that is how you to explain past lives, right? I asked him, "Where does a pine tree come from?" He replied, "A pinecone." "Yes," I responded, "Where did the pinecone come from?" "A pine tree." "And where did that pine tree come from?" "A pinecone" "Yes, that is the cycle, but in that beautiful process called pinecone and pine tree there are times when neither the pinecone nor the pine tree exist yet, where are they?"

So I explained in that lineage called pine tree-pinecone when neither of them are created yet that the IDEA or potential of them does exist for them to be created. You are like that as well, before you were created here in this reality as who you are now the IDEA of you existed in the energy that IS. This is where there is the potential for anything to exist at any time and that potential for creation carries with it the created aspects that have existed before. You brought with you into your creation a condition called asthma.

We then talked about the life of the man I was seeing in my vision and the young boy said he had flashes of those memories, that he actually remembered some of that lifetime. He thought they were dreams or that he had imagined them. We then talked about releasing resentment, unhappiness and anger around our limitations and instead focus on the things you could do and already do. This changed the energy in his energy field almost immediately and he was even able to pet and hug my dog before he left without experiencing any asthmatic distress. It did not 'cure' his asthma but it did assist him and give him some understanding that he has some emotional control over it.

This is the power of identifying and moving the energy in your energy field and affecting it with a higher, faster vibration. This why it is so important to understand vibration and how fast or slow things vibrate.

Past life energy-healing is all well and good but more importantly THIS life energy is of more prime importance. You are living this life so it is to your advantage to first deal with the experiences you have had in this current tangible form. Deciding to heal from the events you have experienced in this life is what will change how you are feeling in that most important of moments, now.

Healing is about perspective. We have only ever really experienced our life from a first person point of view so we only see it from one perspective. The other people involved in the experience are all seeing it from their own point of view and these differing points of view rarely match 100% because each person is bringing their own ideas, beliefs, and truths to the experience.

Interviewing people who witnessed a crime has proven this concept many times, as everyone remembers different aspects of the incident based on their personal experiences and sometimes they even see things that weren't there.

Their memories are almost instantly affected by their own ideas, experiences and thoughts around the incident. Therefore, we think we are remembering everything that happened to us perfectly when in reality we are only really remembering the emotions not the details.

Because we have this beautiful glitch in our system, we can go back into the experience and change our perspective, re-script it and draw new conclusions to let go of an old feeling and replace it with a new one. This must be done with a higher faster vibration or it will not affect the ice cubes in a way that they need to be affected.

For example we cannot go into a negative life experience and bring more anger or resentment to it because that would be like adding more freezing water, it will not melt the ice cube but rather add more density to it creating an even larger ice cube. This is why staying angry and resentful toward someone or an experience cannot heal it. You just keep making a bigger ice cube.

You will need to change the vibration of how you feel about it and you will need to change your perspective to a higher or faster vibration. This can be achieved through bringing in the energy of forgiveness, understanding, and compassion or by creating a new and higher feeling around it, which is like applying steam to the ice cube. Now you have changed the vibration of the energy and it often heals within moments.

An example of this happened when I had a client who had his masters in counselling and his speciality was troubled teens. He came to me because he was experiencing some life challenges around authority.

I asked if he knew the root of his anger and resistance and he said that it stemmed from his relationship or lack thereof with his father. I told him that as long as he held this anger and resentment that he would continually create it in his life experience and that the only way to alleviate it would be to change how he felt about his father. Of course, professionally he knew this but that doesn't mean it is an easy process to do and he stated that he just didn't think that was possible.

There is nothing I like more than a healing challenge so I asked if he was open to allowing me to assist him and see what we could achieve and he agreed. I very carefully set out to change the energy around his feelings toward his dad. I had him close his eyes and visualize his dad and 'assess' him as he would one of his teens and then I asked him to now see his dad as a client, would he refuse that client his assistance? He is a very compassionate and effective counsellor and I could feel his energy change immediately as he perceived his father in this new and different way with compassion and understanding. As he realized the shift was occurring he opened his eyes looked at me with a grin and said, "Well played Tanis, well played."

Whether we are moving energy that is rooted in a present life experience or a 'past life', one of the most important aspects is identifying where in our energy field these are rooted. In the next chapter, I want to focus on the parts of your vehicle that hold these energies in place so that you can perceive them...your bodies.

Chapter 3
You're Talking my Body Language

"I find I no longer have the luxury of being sick. I cannot ignore the messages my body sends me like I used to. It's like ignoring the voicemails on my phone they just stay there waiting to be dealt with piling up until they become unmanageable and inflamed."

~ Personal journal entry 2006

Yup I said bodies – plural. I believe we operate out of four bodies: the Spiritual or Mind-Body, the Emotional Body, The Mental Body and lastly the Physical Body.

Of these four bodies, the spiritual, mental and emotional bodies are not tangible and are composed of purely energy too light to perceive as solid so naturally you can't have surgery on these bodies. The physical body is the only tangible/dense body we possess so I believe that any tangible symptom or condition begins in the energy bodies and then when the energy becomes dense enough it will show up in the physical body.

It's like the dandelions on your front lawn; the part of the flower above the ground represents the physical body while below the surface the roots correspond to the emotional, spiritual and mental bodies. Everything grows from the root up so by the time it hits the physical body it has already existed in the other bodies. If you only deal with things from the physical level then you haven't got to the root of the problem. I mean if you take a pair of scissors and cut all the dandelions down and then proudly exclaim that you have no dandelions... well that's just crazy talk! You will have brand new dandelions tomorrow that will grow once again from the remaining root.

Let's go more in depth with the definition of each of our bodies. The first is our Spiritual Mind-Body. This is the body that stores all the things you have been taught - from your school, parents, church, and life experiences. This is what I refer to as your motherboard or your operating system, this is the body you access to make a decision, solve a problem or access your moral compass.

This is often very primal and safety oriented and has been put into place by your consciousness to make certain that you learn from your experiences and that you do not touch the fire two hundred times to remember that it is hot. It is a linear timeline of experiences that assist you to have a collective experience rather than a series of unrelated separate events in your life.

This wonderful system helps you retain what you have learned. It is the primal 'fight or flight' response so that you learn from your experiences and create a linear timeline. The problem with this system is that we tend to find a strategy that works in the short term and then continue to apply it throughout our life even after we have changed.

We change circumstances but we do not always change how we deal with the circumstances. We apply the fight or flight principle to everything rather than assess the current situation and choose according to our past beliefs rather than the current situation, this can lead us to continually make the same choices but expecting a different result. For example, perhaps you learned as a child that a temper tantrum got you the result you wanted so you continue this into your adult life, but now it presents itself as stubborn anger or inflexibility and does not have the same consequences as when you were two.

Sometimes we plant a belief in this body and all our subsequent thoughts decisions and solutions are born out of this one belief, teaching or conclusion.

Now what if the belief is an erroneous or self-destructive one – for example, 'my father does not approve of me', which then can become 'males don't approve of me' or 'people don't approve of me' and now 'I don't approve of me.' Each decision and solution you make originates from this single belief and subsequently creates more and more of that energy. At some point because of the sheer number of times you have believed this information and acted on it this compilation of low vibrating understandings could create your life circumstances or a density in the body such as a disease or chronic condition.

This low vibratory thought cannot be traced back to the initial belief that you experienced as a child, but if we were able to follow the thread back through the many decisions and solutions that were created along that thought pattern we would find the root cause was established in a time when we did not have the tools or knowing to create any other idea or belief.

I like to call this type of retrieval of a lesson or belief 'quack grass,' because quack grass appears to be separate pieces of grass but when you get under the surface, you find a web of roots interconnecting them and in fact, many other blades of grass are growing from those roots.

When we decide to go into this body to confront or look at our own personal beliefs we can take the opportunity to see which beliefs or truths we are creating our decisions from and how to create from the moment of now instead. We can utilize our experiences but we must also be aware that previous experience may not be the best way to solve a problem or make decision in this moment.

We are in fact a different person in a different moment creating from this moment and not just automatically operating from our previous experiences. Then we can start consciously choosing and creating in this now moment taking our experiences into account but not blindly operating out of them.

We can consciously decide that our experiences do not have to define us and that we do not need to 'become' our experience we can just experience our experiences.

I often refer to this tendency as 'Whitecourt' to my clients. Whitecourt is a town that lies between my hometown and the closest big city in our province. When going to Edmonton from Grande Prairie you have to go through Whitecourt so I use this analogy to illustrate that Whitecourt is something we go through to get to where we are going. You do not stop and become Whitecourt, you do not take Whitecourt with you, Whitecourt is something that you pay attention to as you go through it but you do often just go through it and carry on in your journey.

Your life experiences can be like that too they do not have to define you; you do not have to become them, just go through and learn from them as you are experiencing them and work to just let them go by. Let them be your Whitecourt.

I will illustrate this with a story of young client I was assisting. She came to me because she felt isolated, alone and unable to make friends or be comfortable in social settings. As we discussed her life experiences, she shared with me that when she was young an adult verbally abused her in her home. I asked what tool she used to get away from that situation and she said she used to hide in her bedroom closet and that helped her avoid those situations.

I pointed out to her that this was a good tool; that it had positive results for the most part, and that because it worked so well then maybe she was still using that tool to avoid unpleasantness in her current situation, but now instead of creating safety she was creating isolation, separation and sadness.

She immediately started to cry because she realized in that moment that she was still hiding from people and that even though she was no longer experiencing the verbal abuse she still feared it. Not only that but she was still applying the same tool from her timeline only now it was providing very different emotional results.

This brings us to the second body, our emotional body. This is the body that I find is most closely linked to our memories and to the autonomic system in our physical body.

At any point in time we are experiencing at least one emotion of some kind be it happiness, anger, betrayal, understanding, compassion, boredom, anxiety, etc.

Because the body's physiological system is so closely related to the emotion it is experiencing it reacts immediately according to the intensity and choice of emotions. An emotion cannot be remembered only experienced so this system cannot always tell the difference between remembering and replaying the experience as a thought or actually experiencing it in the moment, so it reacts to thoughts as well as physical experiences in the same way.

Therefore an experience that brings about the emotion of anger, for instance, when remembered can cause the physical body to go into reaction as though the event is taking place right now.

Imagine that you think about this event or person that makes you angry every day and experience the emotion around that thought. You are now creating chronic conditions because you are constantly revisiting that thought and that emotion, so the body has to react in a physical way accordingly. When your body experiences that stress day after day it can become worn and stressed. There are many stress related conditions that have little or no relief from a medical standpoint and that is because they are emotional body issues.

If we separate the emotion from the event or experience you will be able remember the experience without the emotional reaction and then the body has the opportunity to stay in its present state rather than go into the angry state the thought evokes.

To put a human face on this concept I would like to relate an experience I had with a young man around fourteen years old; he came to me because he was acting out, smoking pot, missing school, and just generally unhappy and angry all the time.

When we started talking about his life experiences, he relayed to me that he had been present when his father died.

He had tried to save him by doing emergency resuscitation until the ambulance and police arrived but they were unable to revive him and he passed. This is hard for anyone to experience and he was no exception.

One thing he and his dad loved to do was hunt and they had bonded in this activity. When the police came to the emergency call they seized all firearms that night and this more than anything was causing a great deal of anger in the young man. He expressed to me how much he hated this one officer involved and if he ever saw him again he would threaten him etc.

I could tell right away that he was using this anger to delay or avoid grieving for his dad; it was somehow easier to be angry than sad. I told him that grieving is a necessary and healthy thing that must be done when we lose someone we love. If we delay or suppress that process, it can cause many physical, emotional, and mental problems.

I told him if he would let me help him to move the energy of the anger then he would be able to grieve and would have a better chance of recovering from this trauma.

He really, really wanted to hold onto that anger for that policeman because he could see that if he moved it out of the way this avalanche of grieving was going to crush him. I assured him that I would support his energy and not allow it to overwhelm him and would assist energetically until he was able to hold the pain on his own.

We went into the experience and we started to reconstruct it in a different way, exchanging the anger he felt toward the police officer with what really mattered which is saying goodbye to his dad. We talked about how strong and brave he was in those moments and what was truly important; not the guns, not the police but how much he loved and how much he cared and that is what his last moments with his dad were expressed as; unconditional love.

This completely changed the energy of the experience and within a half hour when I asked him to describe the police officer to me again, he actually could not remember very many details. We had blasted that iceberg with a whole lot of steam!

What I have found in my experience is that the details of the experience go along with the emotion and so you may find that the experience becomes vague and hard to retrieve because emotion keeps things present and memorable. This is so because once again the emotion is a present moment physiological response so the body has to react in the now moment. The body only knows the now moment; for instance look at your feet because your feet are always in the moment of now they are never in your future or past your physical body is always right there in the now moment. If it is not happening in the same place as your feet are then it is not happening. The trick is to **be where your feet are** as often as you can, to operate from this present moment rather than from an emotional memory or from a belief stored in the spiritual body.

The emotional body is also very intimately linked with your memories; you will remember the emotions attached to the event and these emotions are what keep the details in place. A good way to discover the truth of this is to try to remember what you had for supper a year ago today. Unless you have an eidetic memory, that should be difficult or impossible. Now remember what you did for supper on your birthday or a loved one's birthday. You will have a better chance of remembering those details because you have an emotional attachment to that day so it makes the event easier to recall; just like the memories of traumatic events or experiences they have a lot of detail around them.

One of the ways you can move the energy or detach from the emotional memory is to re-script the event through visualization. Go back into the event and create another outcome or look at it from an altered perspective. We think we remember one hundred percent of the event because it is so clear in our minds. The truth is that we only remember a small portion of the actual events and hang on to the emotion around it. This emotion colours the experience and so we have actually already changed the story and it is no longer completely accurate.

Re-scripting isn't really cheating, rather it is rewriting the story to suit who you are now and not being stuck in a flawed and inaccurate memory. We often experience these events as children and do not have the life experience or tools to completely understand what is happening at the time. It is only through life experience that we can ever really get a clearer picture of what was actually happening in our past and with the other people in our story. I always say that as children, we are given a hand full of screws and no screwdriver meaning we are having and being part of all sorts of experiences, but we did not have the necessary tools to understand the perspective of the things that were happening so we tend to create our own conclusions and these become our truth about the experience. When we reach adulthood we will have the perspective and understanding, but rarely revisit the belief and choose to see it from that now expanded point of view. Re-scripting allows you to go back through the experience as an adult and get a better idea of what was really happening thereby changing the emotional repercussions of the original event.

One of the other strategies I use is to have the person speculate or recreate what the event may have looked like from the other person's point of view, and try to see past the details of the story and see the pain or reason behind the other person's actions and choices.

This is the compassion factor – taking your emotional self out the picture and just observing what they are doing and identifying what made them choose that event or experience. This provides another perspective and often gets the person out of the loop of telling their story from their own perspective over and over and instead creating empathy for another. With empathy comes understanding, with understanding comes compassion, and this creates a new energy around the event and cannot have the same effect on you as it used to.

The next place we are going to explore is the mental body. This is the place where all of our known data is kept: memories, information, sequencing, understanding, communication, etc. It is our giant filing cabinet that holds all of our personal files and it is not just what we are intentionally putting into this body that is there, but ALL the DATA your senses are taking in ALL the TIME.

Every nuance, word, information, sounds, thought, outside temperature, dream everything perceived physically, mentally, spiritually, and emotionally is recorded in our brain. This is such an amazing part of who we are and we do not realize a fraction of what it is capable of or even what it is doing at any given moment.

One thing I have experienced in the evolvement process that can be a lot of work is the process of "changing your mind." This can be a long and arduous journey because once again, your mind is doing a gazillion things and so thoughts and impressions are constantly racing through your mind at a phenomenal speed, and can appear as seemingly random as well.

When we start to consciously **think about what we are thinking about,** we find that it can take a lot of energy to continually monitor our thoughts, choose our words, and deciding what thoughts stay and go can be an exhausting process.

The reality is that you have absolutely no control over what comes into your thoughts but you do have one hundred percent control over what stays.

If you are not certain about the truth of this statement sit down and just try to write down every thought, experience and emotion that is going through your head at any given time and you will find that they are actually quite disjointed, sporadic and random. Though at any given moment we are feeling like we are having a thought process and that we have what we are thinking on lockdown, when in reality we are streaming so much information that we can only be conscious of a small amount of what we are actually thinking.

Getting control of my thoughts and focussing them in the direction I want them to go has been the longest evolvement process I have undertaken yet. It took me years of concentrated purpose to be aware of what I am thinking and to choose thoughts, rather than just allowing my mind to race at a million miles an hour without any conscious selection of what I wanted to keep. I cannot truthfully say that I have achieved a quiet state but I can certainly say I have created a more focused one.

One of the things I often do to consciously decide if I want to keep a thought is to ask myself, "Where will this thought take me?" "If I have this thought a thousand times in a row what would I believe to be the truth?" If I am not happy with the projected result I work to change my thought, notice I said work to change, because the work starts when you decide to let the thought go and then you have remind yourself a hundred times, "I choose to let go of this thought."

This deliberate and concentrated thought process can go a long way to eliminating incessant obsessive thought patterns but I must state that once again it is a process that must be undertaken and is definitely not a quick fix. When a client has moved beyond the emotional and physical healing process of their experiences and they go into the creative process of living their lives consciously, this is where I find that the work must now be done in the mind and in the focus of their thought processes. This is when we shift from that reactive being into that creative being and the mind feels like the last frontier to the freedom of conscious creation, I will elaborate on this more in a future chapter.

Here we are at the final body, the physical body, our amazing physical temple where we house and have our life experience. The function of the physical body is to provide a place for the energetic bodies to communicate with us with a version of body language you may not be aware exists.

Because the other 'bodies' consist of pure energy the physical body is the only tangible way of knowing what is going on in our energetic bodies. It is our "check your engine" light letting you know where you need to go to adjust, release or integrate.

I believe that nothing truly exists solely here it just shows up here. That if we deal with an issue in the energy bodies and completely let it transform, integrate or release, the physical body will let it go and the state of being created by that dense energy can be completely and absolutely released and subsequently disappear from the physical body.

That means everything we are experiencing on a physical level has the potential to be reversed or released. If this is true then the physical body has an untapped ability to regenerate completely. I mean we did originally build ourselves from scratch in utero, that ability to create ourselves must still be present in us somewhere. No one, not even our mother consciously created us, she didn't get up from dinner and say, "I'm going to go create some eyes for this baby." We created ourselves from a single cell into multi-cellular beings; surely, we still possess the innate ability to create things from scratch somewhere in our cells.

We don't yet know what has been put in place to separate us from that realization but if we did, I believe that the physical body would not have to wear out and be recreated. We would not have to trade in the old model for a new model, that we could possibly experience physical immortality or at the very least an extended physical existence.

I believe we already experience energetic immortality so physical and mental immortality where we remember the experiences in our tangible and intangible states cannot be out of our reach, right?! What if we could remember being the pinecone, the pine tree, and the state in between? Isn't it amazing what we could allow ourselves to think if we just let ourselves break free from the limitations we have placed on our own human philosophy?

I am sure that six hundred years ago it would have been impossible for the humans in that experience to imagine talking into a small rectangle in their hand to someone a world away but in our experience, it is an everyday, mundane reality.

Why can't we decide that what we do not believe to be true right now in this moment isn't possible at some point because it was those who stepped outside the possible and went into the impossible that created some of the most amazing inventions we enjoy today?

Allow yourself to explore the possibility that you can change how you feel, what you have experienced, and your physical well-being simply by stepping out of what you think is possible and entertaining the idea of what you previously thought was impossible.

Every chance you get allow your Self to ...Change... Your.... Mind... Let your Self think a new thought, have a new idea and experience what that new thought or idea creates.

Healing and evolving doesn't mean much when it stays in the conceptual stage to truly evolve and heal we must have an experience of that concept.

When I was at the very beginning of my journey into understanding how these bodies are connected and how they affect one another I developed asthma at age 35. I suddenly had asthma when prior to that, I had NO symptoms at all. I went to my health professional she said, "It is asthma, here is the way you deal with asthma," and I was now the proud owner of a puffer and asthma medication.

I have never been keen on or responded very well to synthetic medicine, I usually used my mom's home remedies of eucalyptus, steam, rest, the occasional pain medication, tomato soup, toast and tea to work myself through illnesses. So was definitely not a fan of taking this puffer.

Then I found that the medicine in the puffer brought about very disturbing attacks of anxiety. I had never ever been an anxious person, I usually dug my heels in and fought my way through anything uncomfortable and didn't have many unfounded fears though I am a cautious sort – no roller coasters or rodeos for this girl. After using the puffer for a few months, I one day found myself on the floor of the shower sobbing uncontrollably scared out of my mind for no reason whatsoever after taking a dose of the puffer and I had had enough.

This was right around the time my Mom had found our precious naturopath and so I decided to consult with her about this condition. During my session with her she indicated that in holistic medicine we tend to hold unresolved grieving in the chest (this also accounted for the chronic back pain I had between my shoulder blades). She inquired as to whether I had experienced any deaths in the family or any other loss prior to the symptoms of asthma. None came to mind in that moment but then she said she thought it had to do with where I work, she is an amazing intuitive. She asked what I did for a living and I related what I did, I had taught school mostly Grade One. She asked deeper questions and a story came out of me that I had no idea was sitting in there.

I had a very special young man in my class years ago, he was unhappy and not doing well in Grade One and I kept saying to him, "I am not giving up on you!" We eventually created a special supported relationship and I was able to see him flourish. Years later at age nineteen he was killed in an accident; I attended his funeral and was deeply saddened by his passing. What I didn't realize is that I hadn't allowed myself to grieve in a way that supported how I was connected to him. Even though he was nineteen my energetic connection perceived him as six years old, to my energy bodies it felt like I had lost my little Grade One student.

As we discussed this, I began to cry; my whole body went into a kind of paralysis like when your leg is asleep and after a few minutes that subsided and I have never to this day had another symptom of asthma.

Releasing that trapped grief freed me from the emotional trauma I didn't know was there in my energy bodies creating asthma-like symptoms in my physical body. Not everyone's asthma is going to be rooted in grieving but perhaps a lot of people's may be and if they had access to this kind of healing, they may not have to medicate it.

So how do you begin the process of melting those energetic ice cubes, move beyond the trauma and pain trapped in your energy bodies and start to live your life consciously?

Well weirdly enough you start by creating a virtual HEPA filter...

Chapter 4

Don't Fence Me In –
I've Got That Covered

"Life has a peculiar sense of humour every time I teach a boundaries workshop I have a personal experience of my boundaries being tested. I will have to either work on my own boundaries or stop teaching these workshops!"
~ Personal Journal Entry 2010

One of the most important first steps in healing or evolving the Self is to shift your awareness from the outside world to the inside world and sorting out what is yours and what you may be picking up from others. It is about being conscious of the external vibrations that are bombarding you all the time.

Very few people pay close attention to the emotional and vibrational climate that they are experiencing unless it is very intense so we tend to ignore it most of the time, just moving through our day on autopilot and reacting to whatever shows up like a cosmic game of bumper cars.

This is not healthy or productive in the long term and eventually will become painful. We need to become conscious of the vibrations we are allowing into our field and selecting the ones that serve us and let the others pass us by.

Many people build metaphorical walls around themselves, which is only a short-term solution. The funny thing about walls is that they work both ways; it is true that nothing gets in, but nothing gets out either so now you are knee deep in your own sh*%... well you get my meaning.

Energy is always moving, it does not like to stop and when you try to stop it from flowing, you will feel pain. Like water, energy likes to move or it becomes stagnant. Have you ever observed how much dirt and concrete it takes to hold back a river? Well imagine what you would have to construct to hold back energy!

I like to suggest to people starting their vibrational journey to surround themselves with a virtual HEPA filter so that the energy is able to flow but the things you don't need or want can be filtered out and not reach you.

So how do you create a vibrational HEPA filter?

The first thing that must be let go is your need to be needed. Being motivated by the external world all of the time eventually becomes exhausting and stressful. When we are constantly running to fulfill the needs of others before ourselves, we will eventually run out of energy. It is not about becoming selfish it is about becoming Self First.

You can't feed people with an empty soup pot, you have to stop at some point and make the soup. You will need to incorporate this time into your schedule. It is as important as taking out the garbage because if you neglect to take out the garbage pretty soon your house is filled with garbage, and the same holds true for your psyche. Take time each day to take out your emotional, mental and physical garbage.

Shifting your awareness from pleasing others to pleasing the Self takes time and effort to begin with but when you find the balance between taking care of the Self and others there is no greater feeling than the peace and happiness just this one change can bring.

You will need to identify your boundaries and limitations to see how much you 'need to be needed.' " One of the ways to identify this state is to recognize that anything you do out of 'obligation' is really about being needed. Coming to a task or situation as a choice is much more productive than doing it because you HAVE TO because eventually all that creates is resistance and resentment.

Steve Rother author of "Spiritual Psychology" cites the following as symptoms of someone who has personal boundary issues:

- *Think of everyone else's [needs] before thinking of themselves.*
- *They are a people pleaser.*
- *Have a pattern of attracting master manipulators into their lives.*
- *The most difficult word for them to say is "no".*
- *Pick up thoughts, emotions, feelings etc. and make them their own.*
- *Have difficulty in busy crowded places where there is a lot of mixed energy.*
- *Have had a controlling parent or parental figure – often controls them through illness.*

Having boundary issues doesn't mean you are doing your life wrong, is not a bad thing or a life sentence of course just a quality of being that your soul wanted to experience and then master.

The good news is once you have awareness of these issues you are already well on your way to moving through them. They never really 'go away' but you acquire skills and tools to recognize and manage them. As you become proficient in recognizing them your life will become more balanced and subsequently you feel happier and more in control of your own life.

To master and manage this life lesson one must learn to put one's Self first in line. So often, you think that this will be selfish and vain. You probably can't stand people who are so self-absorbed and rarely conscious of how their actions are hurting others. You are usually very aware when someone is hurting, and notice when someone is being undermined or ridiculed. You would probably champion the 'victim' far more quickly than you would stand up for yourself in the same situation. My guess is that you don't just know what they feel you are FEELING it too. So you try to protect them, try to make them feel better, you feel what they are experiencing very keenly and you try to fix it or make them feel better.

We think taking on someone else's pain or solving their problems for them is being self-LESS when really it is the exact opposite, it is self-ISH. By taking on the problems of others we are really saying we are more capable of solving a problem than they are, we are, in reality, seeing them as weaker and less able to handle their own life experiences.

This is not our intention of course; our intention is to spare them pain and suffering by taking it on ourselves. But, just as it is impossible for us to chew other people's food and sustain them the same is true that we cannot take on their suffering and have them learn and grow from their experiences. Would you willing give your suffering to someone else? Would you say I can't do this and then intentionally put the pain onto your children? This is what you are doing when you are taking something that they need to work out on their own; you are taking the experience of failure or success from them.

When you work through a problem and come out on the other side triumphant and empowered, you have conquered your own pain. This is the reward for working through your own pain. This is what you could be preventing someone from experiencing by trying – yes trying - to do by taking his or her pain. I say trying because truly taking someone else's lesson is impossible. It is their lesson, their experience and you cannot have it for them, you can only share the experience and be right beside them but you cannot have THEIR experience only your OWN experience. You will see it differently because you are different people with different life experiences, soul purposes and ways of processing things. Therefore, when you take another's pain or suffering you are really doing something that is less productive for them and yourself.

Imagine if everyone you love and feel a sense of responsibility for is sitting at a table with a large plate of spaghetti put there specifically by the Universe. Your loved one turns to you and says I can't eat all this spaghetti it is too much, I don't want it, it hurts me, etc. so you eat some of their spaghetti, and the next person does the same, and so on. When you finally get to your own plate of spaghetti, you look down at your plate and you have no more room, no more energy to deal with your plate as you are over full and sick from eating other people's spaghetti. This is what comes from expending so much of your energy on their plates rather than yours. You are eventually going to feel exhausted, tired, frustrated and resentful of assisting others because you never really get to the process of eating your own spaghetti. Then something even more distressing happens. Those people who did not eat their spaghetti did not fully appreciate why it was given to them, so the Universal Energy ups the ante and now they get an even bigger plate of spaghetti so that they cannot avoid the opportunity that first plate afforded them. Now they have even more to deal with in their experience.

This really comes down to your need to be needed and expending your energy on other people's problems rather than your own. How you can best support them is to sit down beside them in front of that plate of spaghetti and say, "I will sit here while you eat your spaghetti and cheer you on. I will not leave your side until that plate is empty and then I am going celebrate your ability and strength to manage and conquer your life experiences with you."

When I started my healing business 99% of my clients had boundary issues. This is because I had them as well and we tend to teach what we need to learn and I had made real inroads on my own boundary issues so I could lead the way so to speak.

I was always running around taking on huge responsibilities that were not my own. I was on this committee and that committee and finishing this and running that and being in charge of this....which isn't a bad thing when you have balance but I didn't. I would say, "Well if I don't do this myself it won't get done, and if I don't volunteer for that it won't happen, and if someone else does that it won't be done right and then I will have to step in and fix it anyway." So I took on more and more until I was angry, resentful and frustrated that no one else would step up and help because I had overstretched myself and all those groups became more important than my own health and happiness. Don't get me wrong I felt important, I felt on purpose, and I did great work and was a valuable member of my community but most of the time what I really was, was exhausted.

I decided to find balance, I quit all my external community work and worked on filling myself up first. I started yoga, meditation, scheduled rest times, massages, and play time with the kids became as important as going to work or volunteering my time. I made sure I was doing at least one thing strictly for myself each day. Other than meditation and exercise there is no perfect thing for filling up your energy quota, you are a unique soul, and what fills you up will be a process of discovery for yourself. Sometimes it is hiding in the bathroom with a magazine for five minutes! But, decide to gift yourself with the opportunity to find out and remember these activities won't always stay the same as you grow and evolve, your needs will change as well. As your energy starts to improve do not let yourself fall back into the old pattern and take on a bunch of stuff because now you feel so much better.

I decided to be very selective about the community projects I included myself in and made certain I did not take on any positions because of my needs, guilt or peer pressure. I chose the ones that excited me and held my interest and when my interest or excitement waned, I gave myself permission to move on to something new.

This selective process benefits everyone; I was happier, my family was happier and the projects I took on did not stress me out and benefitted those I was assisting even more. An added benefit of having and creating more energy was that the mundane day-to-day tasks seemed to get easier and easier to accomplish. I would find I was singing as I did the laundry and was excited to see the kitchen clean after supper. Household tasks were no longer using up my last reserves because I had energy all the time.

The next most important thing to help yourself create and maintain a positive energy filter is to be VERY selective about the energy you have around you. I went on a 'negativity diet' which meant surrounding myself with things that had a high vibration: no watching the news, reading the newspaper, participating in gossip circles, paying attention to judgement statements, eating dull lifeless looking foods. Only reading books and watching TV programs that had inspiring messages, making sure my conversations with others and myself were upbeat, honest and authentic.

Life is going to continue to happen while you do this and you are going to encounter negative energy and difficult situations but when you are trimming the negativity in other areas, these incidentals are much easier to manage.

One of the side effects I noticed both for myself and my clients was that we experienced what I call the great "Friend-ectomy". As I changed my energy to higher faster vibrations certain friends seemed to just disappear from my life, we no longer had much in common and we grew apart. I found that if you do not try to direct it in any way the separation is kind and gentle, if you try to hold on when it is time to part you will get drama and trauma and the separation will often be forced by a negative experience.

I don't want anyone to stay in my life out of obligation; I want all my relationships to be genuine and mutually beneficial. Many people experiencing this would say to me, "But we have been friends for twenty years." I would reply, "That is just long – not necessarily successful." This phenomenon differs when we are talking about family and spouses, obviously these relationships are contractual and these people are in your life for very specific reasons and are tools to help you learn what your soul came here to learn.

People with boundary issues are often very sensitive to how other people are feeling, and sometimes so sensitive that they take on the feelings of others without being aware of it. Have you ever walked into work one day happy and ready to get things done and someone else in the room is unhappy? It doesn't take long for people with weak boundaries to take on this negative feeling and make it their own. All of sudden you are having a crappy day and you think why do I put myself through this every day?

I have even noticed myself doing this in the line up for the till in a grocery store, I am patiently waiting in line and very quickly can start to feel upset and impatient about how the line is moving and who is taking so long and can't people read the limit says fifteen items little Miss Twenty Item Girl!

One thing I know about myself is that I am very patient. You do not teach Kindergarten and Grade One for twenty years and not learn patience. When I am feeling negative things, I have learned to look around as soon as I feel it because someone close to me is feeling all those things and I am soaking them up like a sponge.

The first thing you need to understand is that you cannot really take on the person's feelings; they belong to them not to you. What you CAN do is acknowledge the feeling you are receiving from them; name it, recognize it, then make sure you understand that it is not your feeling it is theirs.

By identifying the feeling and not taking ownership over it you are OBSERVING not ABSORBING. This is the first step to truly lessening your pain and understanding theirs. This is creating a boundary – a boundary where you acknowledge what you are feeling but you are realizing that the feeling you are experiencing is NOT your own – it belongs to someone else – that is good news.

Now that you have done this, you can release all ownership and feel empathy for that person, empathy not sympathy. Sympathy means you step right into the emotion and have it with them; empathy means you acknowledge the identity of the emotion but you do not own it, you just feel it. It is like taking someone's hand. You know that what you are feeling is not your hand but theirs; you don't try to become their hand.

You acknowledge the existence of their hand. Maybe you observe that it is warm, soft, hard or cold but these are just observations, you do not become the things that you are feeling emanating from their hand, you just acknowledge them. This is what you want to do with the feelings you are experiencing from them as well, just observe and identify them but you do not have to become them.

This is how you create energetic boundaries by identifying what feelings are yours and which feelings are not. This takes some practice of course; you have been experiencing the feelings of others since you arrived on this planet and so you are used to thinking that what you are feeling is always yours, I mean why wouldn't you? The feelings are coming through your mind and your body so they must be mine, right? Well the news flash is "NO" they aren't always yours, they are just being channelling through your body. You are just a big ol' antenna picking up all the feelings of others around you.

Remember how I said that emotions can really only exist in the moment of *now;* that you cannot remember a feeling, only experience it. It is also true that healing can only happen in the *now* time as well. So, by acknowledging and separating your feelings from theirs you can start the process of moving through and integrating or healing the feelings that are yours instead of trying to affect theirs.

This can be done many ways but forgiveness of self and others is always a great beginning. By acknowledging and identifying which feelings and issues are yours you now have the opportunity to release and heal your part of the relationship. You cannot heal their part of the relationship – that is their job.

It isn't all bad news; the good, amazing and great news about having this ability is that these sensitivities are a sign that you are a master healer. You have empathic abilities, you are pretty darn psychic and you have the ability to tap into and recognize someone else's emotions and pain. Good news right? No so much you think.

I want to reassure you that when you start defining and creating these boundaries and recognizing what does not belong to you – you are also acknowledging and understanding what the person you are getting the feelings from is experiencing.

This means that you are effective and accurate at recognizing emotional pain. This is what being sensitive and caring is, it means you can feel other people's pain, identify where they need to heal and truly help them through their experiences, not by taking them on but by understanding and acknowledging it. This is an amazing ability.

This is why your soul came here like this, it was so you can help others feel better, that doesn't mean you have to be a formal healer or maybe you do – I don't know. What I do know is that you came here with this sensitivity to help facilitate other people and your Self in healing. Maybe you just lend an ear at coffee time, or you are a councillor, a teacher or a nurse because all your life you have felt called to be in service to others and you care about their well being. What I know to be true is that you are this way for a reason, your soul chose this, and when you can create good healthy boundaries and not take things so personally or absorb others energies and maintain your virtual HEPA filter, you provide a beautiful space of love and understanding for them to walk into.

When you acknowledge and empathize with someone, they feel safe, they feel loved and they feel empowered because someone is listening, someone is caring and they feel valuable and they feel like they matter. You are not trying to 'fix' them you are just acknowledging their state and trusting that they know how to solve their own problems. When you create and maintain your personal boundaries, you are strong enough to stand in your own power, your own energy and just love them, whatever they are experiencing.

I once heard compassion defined as 'fierce grace' when you can help another without losing yourself in the process. This is the peaceful warrior, this is true power, this is pure love and you are a big part of that.

Not only do we experience external boundary issues we also have internal boundaries in place that can stop our forward movement. The most powerful internal limitation we face is fear.

I have always likened fear to fog because it never seems to be right where you are, but rather just out of reach. As you move in fog, the space around you stays clear but the way forward is always obscured and just a few feet away the sun can be shining but you cannot know that unless you move forward in it.

Fear obscures your vision and stops you from moving forward confidently. Often our fears are based on experiences and teachings and sometimes they are not even our own experiential fears but ones passed down to us from others. I have come to know that the only thing ever really standing in my way is myself.

I don't like being bossed or told what I cannot do by other people and have rarely let others decide for me but I can be stopped immediately by my own fear. Sometimes I would tell myself lies and say that an outside force is stopping me but in reality, the only thing that has ever truly stopped me was me.

It is important at some point to stop thinking that the outside world is 'out to get you', 'I can never catch a break' or 'everyone has it better than me' and instead see where you are stopping yourself. What internal fears are you simply unwilling to face? Failure, ridicule, judgement, or maybe you even fear the responsibility of success?

Get real with yourself and see where you are holding someone or something responsible for how you are feeling and use it like a mirror and decide in what ways have you limited yourself. Get out of judgement and opinion as much as you are able, especially in regards to other people's choices.

You have NO control over the outside world only the inside world, that is where your opinions and judgements must be examined for how they serve YOU and no one else. And remember that the truth is a liquid not a solid. What you believe is true today may not be true for you tomorrow so don't get really attached to your current truth.

Six hundred years ago the village would have been entertained by burning someone like me. Now it would be frowned upon, so what changed? Just the truth about whether or not that is ok, as a collective we decide how a thing is going to be perceived and we take that as a solid truth until someone disagrees and then when enough people disagree the collective truth changes.

These are just the first few steps in creating an energetic HEPA filter and consciously changing your Self but you are not living on a deserted island all by yourself. There are people in your life and they play an important part in your evolution, so my advice is to walk softly and carry a big stick...

Chapter 5
Everything is Fun and Games
Until Someone Gets Poked in the I

"Take a picture of your soul and shine it brightly so all may see and awaken to their own divinity. Those who you think reject you have rejected the Self." This channelled message came to me in perfect timing as I am saddened by the rejection of a friend. I want to fix it but to do so I will have to forsake my Self and I cannot do this and still love who I am. It does not serve me in any way to believe their version of me and so I let them go and give myself the freedom to be me.
~ Personal Journal Entry 2011

Getting poked in the 'I' means that someone has shown up in your experience and is causing you discomfort and turmoil. Our natural inclination is to blame them for how we are feeling. Healing is accelerated greatly when we gain an awareness that everyone in your life is there for a/and on purpose. You will begin to understand that both the guy who cut you off in traffic and the kind lady who smiled at you in the grocery store are there to provide you with relativity, with something to bounce your perception of off so that you can more clearly see your Self.

I came to an epiphany one day, realizing that I have never really seen myself...I have seen pictures, a reflection in a mirror, or in the water; I have seen myself through the eyes of others but because my eyes are sunk into my head I have only ever seen a reflection of my Self.

In a reflection there is always a degree of distortion - nothing is ever unadulterated or a true representation. How then can I see my Self more clearly?

I find I can do this if I just close my eyes and feel.

This is me, this is who I am at any given moment, I am what I am feeling, thinking and being. This is an unadulterated version of me; this is who I am being right now. We so rarely do this, and when we do the feelings have to be very intense or triggered by another before we pay any attention to what we are feeling; this is a very reactionary way to live our lives.

It is very common to see people in this world blame the things they are feeling and experiencing on other people or circumstances. The truth is that you are always in charge of how you feel all the time. Feelings can be triggered in you by an external source but you will be the only one feeling what you are feeling. When you want someone to know how you feel they can only do that to the extent of their own experience. The feelings may be similar but they will be unique to the feeler.

One of my favourite sayings is when you point a finger at someone look at your own hand because three fingers are always pointing back at you. When you take full responsibility for how you feel and know that you are in charge of that it gives you the opportunity to change how you feel. If someone else was in charge of how you feel that makes you powerless to change your feelings.

This is often the cause of a lot of the stress in our lives, that we feel that someone or something else is in charge of how we feel; our boss makes us feel inadequate, our parents make us angry, our partner doesn't understand our needs and so on – it then feels like the feeling is being imposed upon us.

What if you decided how you wanted to feel? What if you made a conscious choice what you wanted to feel in that experience? What if that feeling was productive and served you in a positive way rather than in a restricted and powerless way.

It is possible to do this – it is possible to change how you feel. You can do this by understanding that the person or situation is there for your benefit, to point you to the things inside of you that are creating this condition.

We live in a relative world and we cannot have the experience of who we are without it, as Neale Donald Walsch says in Conversations with God, *"You only are what you are relative to another that is not. It is only through your relationship with other people, places and events that you can even exist."*

We must understand the purpose of relationships with others to truly understand ourselves. We must learn to use relationships to grow and evolve rather than play bumper cars with people and events hoping we come out of the experience without too many bruises and broken bits.

This goes back to the catalyst I was speaking about in Chapter One. This is where we can use the people and circumstances we are experiencing to our advantage.

I like to call the people who trigger a lot of emotion and resistance in me **wound pokers** because they have come into my life and provoked me into reacting and now I have to protect and defend myself. When you are poked, you will often react with statements such as, "Hey that hurts!" "Stop it!" "Stop poking me!" "You hurt me!" "How could you?" "Don't you love, respect, and care about me?" "What gives you the right to hurt me?" Does any of this sound familiar?

Well you have just met your wound poker. You have met someone who is present in your life to assist you in deciding who you are in relation to them.

They will go by many names; spouse sister, brother, mother-in-law, adversaries, boss, Dad, Mom, Bob. But, they are all present for the same reason; they are here in your relative world to assist you with creating who you are in that moment. These are your soul contracts the people you have energetically placed very carefully in your life experience so that you will gain a deeper understanding of your Self.

I want to talk about your relationship with them in terms of creating boundaries and limitations because if your personal HEPA filter isn't up and in place, you will feel the effect they can have on your energy. These people constantly take advantage of those weak personal and energetic boundaries you experience. They bully you in school, they yell and punish you at home, then you marry one and they physically, mentally, and emotionally abuse you as well.

They are your friends who are always going through some trauma or drama. Sometimes they aren't even in your life all the time but chance encounters; they are the rude receptionists, ticket counter agents, and your kid's teachers. They are energy suckers and you instantly feel tired, weak and disempowered around them. Sometimes the boundary isn't breached with something negative but rather the manipulation can appear positive, they are always in some sort of distress, they are ill, or they stroke your ego and tell you how vital and important you are to their happiness so much so they cannot live without you. This is still a form of manipulation.

They do serve a noble purpose and that is to FORCE you to create a boundary because at some point you will get so fed up you will finally just draw a line in the sand and say do not cross this, this is my limit, this is where you cannot go. Then the marriage fails, you leave home, or you stop seeing those friends or they change their behaviour and respect your boundary but this is a boundary! Yeah! You created a boundary!

That is why you are always being pushed, that is why these people constantly come into your life because you made agreements with them on a soul level to have them play "bad cop" and come into your life and push you and abuse you. Until you are so fed up that you create a boundary, hold the line, and decide who you will be in the experience.

Now that we understand their purpose we can look at these people, release our victim status and say to ourselves, "Thank You, for pushing me so hard I had to do something about it."

Think of the love they have had to sacrifice at a soul level so you will hate and resent them enough that you can create that energetic line. What a harsh role to play, what a soul sucking assignment, when what their soul really wants is to be loved and honoured by you. Instead, they have to create all this chaos so you can learn to create and maintain a boundary, what an amazing sacrifice.

This is not a one-way experience. They too came here to learn what not loving yourself feels like, what feeling the lack of personal power feels like in a situation where they need to overpower everyone else in the hopes of creating a power they do not feel deep down inside their own psyche.

These are the soul agreements you have made and wouldn't it be nice to just release all that hate and resentment and thank them instead so they can carry on with their soul assignment? Now when you get poked you can recognize that one of your wounds has been pointed out to you and you get the opportunity to heal it. Now you can just let them go by loving and accepting them as they are rather than holding blame and resentment toward them.

You don't have to live or work with them; try to make them understand your needs and you certainly aren't responsible to "fix" them anymore. You can just let them go about their business learning what they came here to learn and you can learn what you came here to learn as well.

You have been the wound poker for others as well. You have come to push someone to make a boundary and decide whom they are that is the beauty of the human experience.

So when your next wound poker shows up (and they will!) say aloud or in your head, "Ouch, I didn't know that wound was there, thank you for pointing that out, looks like I got some learning to do", and carry on.

Now you do not need to hold anyone outside of you responsible for how you are feeling on the inside. This is when you can close your eyes and stop dealing with that distorted reflection of yourself the one who reacts to what others think of you and start working with the authentic self, the one who is deciding how they want to feel.

One of my favourite quotes from Neale Donald Walsch is, "*What is happening is happening but who you are in what is happening is up to you.*"

So how do you go work on your Self? How do you get poked and then take charge of how you feel?

Well you go within – because if you don't go within you go without.

Chapter 6

Developing Your Sixth Sense: I See Live People... They Don't Know They are Alive

"You all have what you call 'psychic power.'" It is, truly, a sixth sense. And you all have a "sixth sense about things." Psychic power is simply the ability to step out of your limited experience into a broader view. To step back. To feel more than what the limited individual that you have imagined yourself to be would feel; to know more than he or she would know. It is the ability to tap into the larger truth all around you; to sense a different energy.

~ *Neale Donald Walsch,*
Conversations With God, Book 3

Healing from external influences and past experiences can take a lot of time and energy. Changing how you see your Self and those around you is not an insignificant endeavour. It takes a great deal of self-examination and often a heroic effort to commit to and sustain such a task.

You will experience many changes internally and externally throughout this process and not all of them will be pretty, but do not despair as the result is truly worth the effort.

What we are really doing is examining the stored energy that has been weighing us down with accumulated density and deciding to transform it to a higher vibration thereby changing the effect is has on our bodies. This takes us into a different vibration or frequency and subsequently a lot of shi'f't happens.

Remind yourself as you move through the many shifts you experience that you are embarking on a personal journey into conscious creation and celebrate that process often – make it as joyful as you can. I mean what is there not to be happy about? You are letting go of all that emotional and energetic garbage that weighs you down and stops you from feeling alive.

This is when we go from just surviving our life to thriving in it. We are becoming not just pathfinders but path-makers. We are conscious creators of our own life experience and there is nothing more important to celebrate and be joyful about than that.

Once we have taken the time and energy to clean out our spiritual closet we can start to live our life in a more conscious way and to do that we will need to go within, not just to heal but also to move from reacting to the things that are happening but to respond to them instead.

There are tools and processes you can use to achieve this especially now that you have that amazing filter in place. You can now use that big antenna that you have been using to absorb all that energy from around you, and instead use it to access that stream of Universal Energy and collective consciousness that has just been waiting to assist and guide you.

It's time to go to the spiritual gym and start to work and flex your psychic muscles; wake them up and learn to trust the information you receive from an internal universal source.

This internal source is called your intuition or sixth sense. Everyone has this source and we were in touch with it more as a small child. In fact, this is the part of the brain you used to use to pretend or imagine. Over time, you learned not to trust it because those around you told you that it isn't real, you're just pretending or making it all up and so you began to lose the ability to trust the information coming through this part of the brain.

Consequently, as we age we tend to rely less on this internal source of knowing, and more on our mental body or learned behaviour. Somewhere along the line we are taught that unless the information we are getting can be substantiated by another it isn't real; that the things you are feeling in your body or seeing in your mind's eye are not real because no one else can see or feel them.

Thank goodness some brave souls decided to risk themselves and step out of the status quo and challenge those arbitrary rules that were, for the most part, created out of fear. If no one ever had the courage to step outside that proverbial box we would still be wandering around in the field carrying a big stick and grunting.

Like with anything else, going too far one way or the other creates instability and dysfunction. What we want is to strike a balance between totally relying on what we have learned and what we intuitively know. If we rely too heavily on our mental body or what we have learned exclusively from outside sources, we can become overly skeptical, question everything or require proof all the time. This creates a low level of trust and we can spend a life time trying to find 'proof' and then never really trusting the proof we found because of our own insecurity and fear of being wrong.

On the flip side, having only faith and no discernment can be just as debilitating. Believing everyone and everything with very little thought or on blind faith can leave you open to manipulation and oppression.

If you are not applying the information in a practical way, or blinding acting on every little thought or feeling that comes through without taking into account that these fleeting feelings are part of a bigger picture or someone else's truth, you are like a puppet. This is how despots and dictators can become so powerful.

We have both a brain that learns and accesses that universal information for a reason and that is to use them like a team in a magnificent co-creation. A good balance is achieved when you allow information to come into your awareness through all channels and then decide on a personal level whether or not that is a truth to you based on what you feel, what you are experiencing, and the result you want.

It is an important distinction that the truth does not come from an external source but rather will be decided by you at an internal level. That is why people have differing truths. Everyone has access to the same information but one will feel it is true and another will not.

Everyone is given information from all kinds of sources; deciding what your truth is for you, will be up to you. Get a good sense of what it feels like to experience a truth, a truth is often felt like sensation not unlike the sound of gong; it has a resonance and vibration so pay attention to that feeling so you will recognize it.

This is what I call putting information through your, "truth filter" and practicing personal discernment. Remember also that what you believe to be the truth now will change as you grow and evolve so don't get too attached to your truths because truth is a liquid, not a solid. Stay flexible and discerning so you can change your mind when more information becomes available to you.

Let's explore how the information can come in through your intuitive centers:

It is hard to see yourself clearly, so the messages or sensations associated with these tools are more easily perceived when you are assisting others. So when you first begin to develop them, having a like-minded 'open to some amazing stuff' kind of healing-buddy that will help you experience these amazing gifts as you both will grow immensely from the co-creation.

Clairsentience (Clear Feeling)

This is the information you were streaming unconsciously before the placement of the filter when you were picking up the energy fields of the people around you. This sensitivity makes the emotions and energies of others available to you and often you can feel it in your own body, but rather than absorbing it you will now observe it with the intent to assist the other in identifying it and its cause.

This is the most pre-dominant "Clair" I use in my healing practice. I feel pain, pressure, or sensation inside my own body from the emotional energy field of the person I am assisting. I use my body like a map to ascertain what the other person is experiencing without really needing to ask them.

When I am working with someone and experience their pain in my body, this lets me know to ask them about issues in that area of their body. I also use this indicator to monitor when they have moved the energy because as soon as it gone from my body I know it is clear from their energy field.

Lots of times you can get information that is only in their energy body and they may not be experiencing it yet, which means that the pain or issue is still at the energetic stage and hasn't presented itself in a physical way so do not discount your intuitive knowing. I have learned through experience not to expect confirmation of this from the person because I trust what I am getting and if it is still in the energy stage, they may not yet even be aware of it.

Once the area of the body or emotional issue held in that body are identified, I use whatever healing techniques necessary to address the problem area.

Another aspect of this sensitivity is getting a strong feeling such as an overwhelming sense of sadness or anger. You are now tapping into emotions that the person is moving through or has experienced.

This is when the conversation becomes an important part of the process so that awareness of what they are holding and how it is affecting them is understood.

I then release any residual pain out of my own body by acknowledging that it is just a message AND NOT MY RESPONSIBILITY. They are just empathic and intuitive feelings. Encourage the one you are assisting to share their experience of your accuracy as this validates your information and is great at building your confidence and trust in this *Clair*.

Clairvoyance (Clear Seeing)

This is when you see beyond the physical. Clairvoyant abilities can occur in the form of visions, both still and moving internal images and in seeing people who have passed.

These are usually processed in your "mind's eye" or "third eye". For me, the best way I can describe how they present themselves is they are like remembering an old photograph. They happen very quickly but I have a lot of detail around that fleeting image.

I usually get clairvoyant information when I need to ask about someone who has passed or people they are processing emotional issues about.

I also get images of a certain age and then know to ask what was happening in their lives at that age, as this usually indicates a trauma or other catalyst in their life experience. When they relay the information I will get an intuitive 'hit' meaning that the event or circumstance they are talking about has a lot of energy around it. This starts out as a subtle knowing and strengthens with use.

It is important to build an internal personal 'symbolic dictionary' for your clairvoyant visions, as very often what you see is symbolic in nature and not literal. As you practice this ability, you will develop a set of symbols that represent something to you, so you can more easily interpret the messages and have a clear conversation with your intuition. For example, I will see an image of my grandmother in my mind and then I know to ask about the person's grandparents.

The other circumstance that comes up as clairvoyance for me is when I am helping someone process around past life issues, this helps to pinpoint the time or place in history or the situation that has been left unprocessed energetically, usually through awareness of the event most often a death or traumatic situation.

Past life energy usually presents itself when there is a parallel to something happening in this lifetime so we can gain an understanding of the current event or scenario and work through any unresolved emotional trauma across the linear time line.

Claircognizance (Clear Knowing)

This is when you have information for a person or situation that you could not have previously known through interaction or experience with that person. It is when the information that is needed is instantly available.

This can also be used for channelling or premonitions. We all have access to any information that we need at any given time; when we practice and trust the information given to us, we start to hone this skill.

I find that there are times when my mouth is saying something even though the thought wasn't really in my mind before I said it. It is not as if I was formulating the answer and then relaying it, the words just bypassed my brain and came out.

I love when that happens because it is usually very straight forward and not muddled by my human thought processes. This is usually that gong-like truth that is spoken. I will be sharing how to develop your channelling abilities later on in this book.

Clairaudience (Clear Hearing)

This is when you are hearing voices, music, and other sounds that have no physical source. This ability can also be accompanied by a high-pitched whine or 'sound void' that come into your ears every now and then.

It is this type of message that is most often explained away by logic. "I must have been hearing things!" Which is, of course, correct, you are. You are getting an audible message to pay attention, to make note or take notice.

Lots of people experience this message. When in life or death situations, many will say I heard someone say, "Turn left, stop or do not go in there", these types of life-saving situation messages are usually very clear and attention getting.

I also have experienced this type of message when the person had said something yet I hear something different from what they said, so I will repeat the information and they will say, "I didn't say that?" The message I heard usually helps me identify an area that needs healing or attention.

This is also experienced as an inner voice, what you may have called your conscience, the dialogue you have in your own head with yourself. This is when you get information via that voice and realize later that the information was pertinent and maybe you could have paid better attention to the message and avoided a situation. This happened to me once when I was leaving the house and I saw my son's bike in the garage, (which is always there), and this time I thought I should lock that up, but I just carried on and was regretting that decision when later that day we noticed it was gone.

Another clairaudient message is when you get a 'song worm' that is when a certain song or phrase will "get stuck" in your head, this is a message too. Pay particular attention to the lyrics to see if there is information or a message there for you or think about whom the song reminds you of, or a time in your life when that song was pertinent to pinpoint what information is coming to assist you.

If you are having the experience of a lot of ringing in the ears for no apparent reason you can acknowledge the messages by just expressing gratitude this will often allow the information to be downloaded intuitively. When I hear it (I get this symptom a lot) I silently say thank you for this information, take a deep breath and trust that when it is pertinent I will be able to access it. I rarely hear things along with the buzzing but information will come to me later.

Clairessence or Clairaliance (Clear Smelling)

This occurs when you smell things that have no physical source.

This is an interesting sensitivity because the amazing thing about smell is that it connects very quickly to memories. When you smell a familiar smell, you can access the people or situation immediately.

This makes it a powerful intuitive tool, as the message is usually very clear and concise. Like clairaudience, it is easy to explain it away and find a logical explanation for the smell, but when you accept that it is in fact a psychic smell you usually have a very clear understanding of the situation you are integrating or the person you are in contact with.

I have a super story to go with this one! For a few days I would catch a whiff of this rancid smell, and even though I did a massive clean of everything I could think of, I couldn't find the source. I asked my husband and sons if they smelled anything they kept saying no. One day my sister Shar stopped by to pick me up to play cards at a friend's, walked into the house and said, "Oh my! What in the world did you have for supper that smells so terrible?" I was so excited she could smell it! She too said it smelled like rancid meat, so I took that as confirmation that I wasn't crazy. Later that night we were both very ill and so we called my other sister Shari, she is a medium and an excellent resource when you need details about past life events. She works in a bakery and when we called her there she immediately said, "What the heck is that horrible smell!" She told us she was seeing us both afflicted with the plague and that we were clearing energy being held in our energy field around our dying and relationship in that lifetime. There was just no other explanation for what we smelled, it had no physical source and of course she would not be able to smell it in a bakery three kilometres away. This experience demonstrated to me the power of what I like to call a *'psychic smell'* and often ask people, "Do you smell that?" Just in case I'm getting a message.

Clairambience (Clear Tasting)

When you taste things without having eaten it, this is clair-ambience.

This is a lesser known "clair" to me, as I haven't had much personal experience of it myself. In my estimation, it would be like clairessence where you can be tempted to explain it away with a logical explanation, but like a psychic smell it is probably very clear and concise with the information you have accessed.

When you get this message, use your own experiences to remember what the situation or the specific people are associated with a taste; this will help you in your understanding for yourself or the person you may be working with.

***

These are "psychic tools" to help you tap into and read the messages in both your own and other people's energy field. Be mindful that other people's energy fields are private, just like their underwear drawer, so it is spiritual etiquette to wait to be invited into their energy and give them information.

All the "clairs" are intuitive tools to help you remember and identify experiences in you or another that have helped to create density in your energy field. Remembering brings awareness to that density so that you can move through it, integrate it, change the perspective, or heal it so that you no longer hold a negative or limiting thought around that situation or person and then you no longer have the effects of that density in your physical and emotional body.

We want to be in awareness of these dense areas because even if we feel like they have happened in the past and are no longer relevant, the truth is that they still exist energetically and can affect you if you do not deal with them.

People come to a healer or seek to heal because of emotional and physical pain or because they are dealing with disease or depression. These intuitive tools are opportunities to access a higher understanding or a different perspective on the situation.

There is a process that you must go through to build trust and accuracy in interpreting and sharing your intuitive information. This comes with experience and frequent use.

That is why it was of great benefit to me when I was building and working my intuitive muscles to be able to work with others in a non-judgemental, supportive way. We formed a group of like-minded people and we met once a week and played with our abilities, honing and growing them with hands-on experience. This is how we conducted our 'Healing Circles'.

We placed one person on a massage table; they indicated what they wanted to work on or they allowed the rest of us to 'pick up' that information via our intuition.

We would stand around the table with hands on or above (whatever your preference) and then we tuned into our 'Clairs' and using the information that came through to assist them with whatever they came to the circle to uncover or gain clarity around.

It is important that no information be dismissed or deemed unimportant because at first messages will be vague and often unsupportable while some are strong and the person can validate them for you. As you grow your abilities your accuracy will improve, but discounting the messages can create a distrust or embarrassment, which can shut down the channels and make you lose confidence in your ability just as being told we are just pretending did to us as a child.

Support and honour one another and be discerning. You do not have to believe everything or act on all the messages; just allow them to flow and choose the ones that feel right to you as the person receiving the assistance.

All messages from universal guidance are loving and supportive. If information gets critical or angry, like it is venting you have gone into fear and back into the human construct. Universal Energy is never this way because it is 'all that is' meaning it comes from an absolute state of being with no polarity. Judgement exists only in a relative world, one with polarity where the concept of right and wrong exist. Universal Energy, Source, God, Essence does not fear or get angry as these emotions are exclusive to the human experience which runs on the illusion that we are separate from one another.

It may sound strange, scary, or even ridiculous that you have the ability to get messages from the expanded Universal part of who you are especially because we were often raised to fear or ridicule the 'voices in our head.' In his usual joking manner, my Dad would always say talking to yourself was okay but when you started answering yourself, you're crazy!

Time to get crazy!

Chapter 7

Sticks and Stones Can Break my Bones But Powerful Words Will Heal Me

"As I am writing my book I revisit my personal journals and I find my first working journal and I see that every day for more than a year I worked with ME. I wrote down affirmation after affirmation diligently changing thoughts, beliefs, and conclusions about my Self until they became my reality. Even now, I find myself immediately changing a thought that does not serve me in a positive way. Affirmations have become my habit, my practice and my process defining in each moment who I AM and who I choose to BE."

~ Personal journal entry 2014

I am going to revisit an earlier topic and remind you again of the different bodies we work with: the spiritual mind-body, emotional body and the mental body. All of these bodies have no tangibility, you cannot have surgery on them, they are energetic in nature.

I believe that everything we have experienced and all of our issues are held in these three bodies, and because they are composed of energy the issues held in them can be difficult to perceive or access unless you have a vast working knowledge of energy. They have to show up somewhere so this is where the physical body comes into play and becomes our "check your engine" light.

Just like the warning light in your car, your body lets you know where the density is stored, and when you know how to interpret the message you can go in and work on that physical symptom from an emotional and spiritual angle as well as supporting the physical symptom.

This is where Louise Hay will become your best friend ever! In her book *"You Can Heal Your Life"* she gives great practical exercises to heal yourself, and they are all very effective and will absolutely help you heal the traumas trapped in your bodies. At the end of the book is an appendix that cites different symptoms and parts of the body and what they mean from an emotional standpoint and then gives a new thought pattern or affirmation to help replace the old thought or pattern.

She also published a book called *"You Can Heal Your Body"* which is this appendix on its own and there is an 'app' for mobile devices that has the same information. Becoming familiar with what your physical symptoms mean in an emotional and spiritual sense expands your view of why you are experiencing this in relation to your present or past events. This brings in another perspective, which in turn changes the energy and therefore the result of that energy.

I believe nothing exists only in the physical body and that it exists as an energy and 'shows up' in the physical body. If we can heal it in the energy 'bodies' it can literally disappear from the physical body because the root or sponsoring energies have been resolved and can no longer create that symptom or condition (or ice cube).

How do we do that? How do we go from reading it in a book and then changing or resolving the energy around it enough to let it go so it completely disappears from our physical body?

We are a cellular being. We are made up of trillions of cells that continually die off and regenerate and for us to remain intact the mother cells pass on information to their daughter cells so that memories and form are retained. We actually are a completely different person in the cellular sense every few years.

Unlike our human mind, our individual cells have no judgement attached to the information that they store; they do not see information as positive or negative, it is just information to them.

What we perceive as "negative" information has more density than "positive" information. This being the case we vibrate slower when our cells contain "negative" information, thus we have the potential to create pain or dis-ease. When we choose to replace these negative or dense beliefs with positive or light beliefs, we are essentially creating a lighter, healthier way of being at a cellular level.

Have you ever wondered, I mean truly wondered, why words hurt our feelings? How can someone just say something to me and it hurts me in a physical or psychological way?

I believe that all words carry a frequency and how the body, mind and spirit accept that frequency creates our experience of it. If we do not give any power to the words, by that I mean we simply do not agree with them on any level, we will have a significantly different result than when we agree with them on some level. If they bring up energy from our past experiences our mind-body will immediately go into the same emotions that it had at the time.

Let's use the example of an experience or trauma in childhood; the trauma is stored and remembered by the physical body, the mental body, the emotional body and the spiritual body. This means that we move through the physical experience but can retain or store the trauma in each of the other bodies.

Eventually our mental body may 'forget' it and it no longer lives in our day-to-day consciousness, but it can still sit in the emotional and spiritual bodies without our conscious awareness. Eventually these stored traumas can cause dis-ease or pain even though we have no physical memory of them. In other cases, the mind does not forget the trauma and you continue to live through the event emotionally every time you think about it. Remember from previous information that the physical body is very closely linked to the emotional body. When the incident is still so attached and revisited by the mental body all the time, this dense emotion has less chance of being forgotten and more opportunity to create dis-ease and painful physical and emotional symptoms because the mind is constantly re-telling the story and bringing up the emotions, which in turn affect the physical body.

One of the ways we can release these trapped traumas from the mind and emotional bodies and become lighter, vibrate higher, and improve our health is through a process I learned called "Clearing," which is to identify our issues and then "clear" them. Over time I have come to realize that none of my issues are really "cleared," meaning they are not expelled from my body (in reality there is nothing truly outside my body from an energetic point of view). I have found that the process is better described as **integrated or transformed**.

Every issue and trauma that my body has stored and remembered is an experience and experience is what my soul came here to do. If I were to seek to just expel it from my body with no awareness of why it was created in the first place, I dishonour the reason I kept it.

I kept it because it is important for me to learn and grow from it. I use "integration" or "move through" now instead of clearing because this honours my life experiences, and makes my life experience a creative one that I am fully involved in and am not perpetuating or creating the reality of being a 'victim' of outside forces.

As a modality, "Integration" is a way for us to take responsibility for our own body/health issues. I visualize the cells in the body as 'banker's boxes' where we continually add things to them and the storage box just accepts them without judgement of any kind. As I move through my life experiences, I am adding energy to my banker's boxes. I am adding either dense or light energy but I am always adding energetic information.

If your banker's boxes have accumulated a lot of dense-heavy energy in them, it is like carrying heavy stones around with you all the time; eventually the bottom of the box can be compromised by the weight and start to weaken and sag, and then the things we stored in there weaken the cell and will become noticeable in the form of a physical symptoms such as pain, dis-ease or depression.

This is the same with an emotion or experience you have set aside and hoped never to see again. It eventually finds its way back into your consciousness and you will need to deal with it. This is where emotional and energetic healing is necessary to transform the stored information.

It is identifying and working through the emotional components that will ease the physical discomfort in our body. Integrating is essentially identifying and finding those areas of your body that are holding onto information from your past. When we choose to replace negative or dense beliefs with positive or light beliefs we create a lighter, healthier way of being in ourselves at a cellular level. We are choosing to sort through and remove the dense/negative energy stones from our banker's boxes. This will create a new result in the body. As you collapse the energetic pathways that created the previous condition new pathways are created because they carry a higher frequency, now they can create a new result.

There are ways for you to identify the stored emotions in your body or in your psyche. The most effective is to identify the root cause or experience that created it. Once the root causes have been identified, you can then gain an understanding of the gift each experience brought to you and integrate it into your being, thereby releasing the negative effect it is having on your body, mind or spirit.

One of the intuitive gifts I have worked to hone is my ability to read and track the information or pathways that were made in the energy bodies. This helps identify when or how that 'root' was formed in your linear time line, identifying the age or circumstance can really assist in zeroing in on the experience that is being stored.

I believe anyone can do this with time and practice. Using the 'Clairs' will allow you to pinpoint with considerable accuracy where the root was created. Using the body like a map to find the root cause is also a great way to start this process and this is where Louise Hay becomes a vital component.

"You Can Heal Your Life" is one of the most important books in my repertoire. It is one of the first healing books I read, and it explained so clearly how our emotional baggage affects our physical body. I was even more excited to learn that we can release the effects of these trapped emotions and heal our bodies ourselves. I began to use her lists whenever I experienced symptoms of the body, sought to relate the probable cause to events in my experiences, and then used the new thought pattern or affirmation to transform it in the form of repeating it like a mantra.

I use this book daily in my healing practice and carry it in my purse for quick reference, as most people are very willing to share their physical woes. Often I will whip out the book and assist those who are willing to go deeper than the pain they are feeling and discover the reason behind the pain. I am a total hoot at parties (sarcasm intended here)!

In all seriousness, I did have to learn to wait until the person showed a real interest in the process before going into it too deeply. Healing is a very private, deeply transformative process. There can be a lot of pain and disclosure involved, and when emotional trauma is released, being in a safe supportive environment is much more conducive to healing than the office Christmas party.

So how do I use Hay's book to heal? The obvious first step is to read it and do the exercises OR just pick it up each day, turn to a page and do the exercise or read the passage with the intention that it has a message for you.

As I've already discussed, my favourite way to use the book is to reference the body index at the back and identify the physical manifestations of the trapped emotions; looking at the probable causes and seeing if any of the suggestions resonate with me.

I then journal or discuss the information with a trusted person that matches the probable cause and dig for the deeper reasons behind the symptom. By bringing the experience to your consciousness, this will help you realize what past event you have stored is unresolved.

This is the most important part of the process for me. It is when I get to look at the experience with a fresh and new perspective perhaps choosing to see it from a more loving place and to take the chance to understand or forgive the other people involved in the process. We must bring in that higher, lighter vibration at this point or we will not be able to transform the issue. It is imperative to find a new perspective and let the old perspective go because the old perspective is causing the pain.

The new thought pattern or affirmation is the next vital part of the process. Read and repeat the affirmation OUT LOUD. This engages more senses. Now do not just read it, FEEL it! I do not allow my client or myself just to give the sentence lip service. I want them to go inside and feel that new thought, embrace it, and put it firmly in their banker's box and ousting that old, dense, negative thought. Sometimes I will have them write it down and say it as a mantra until they begin to believe it or at least hear and think it so much they have no choice.

This part of the affirmation process is important, otherwise you are just repeating sentences; which is kind of like being punished by writing lines you are just saying something over and over hoping it's true but it isn't really changing how you feel. Changing how you feel is the most important aspect of healing. As I have said before you can't remember a feeling only experience it, so when you do not have the feeling you are NOT experiencing it. We want to FEEL the truth of the affirmation.

I was working with a sixteen-year-old client and she was experiencing low self-esteem, ridicule and being excluded by her peers. We talked about creating an affirmation that she could have on default when she was thinking or experiencing criticism, and she suggested the affirmation, "I am beautiful." I asked her, "Do you believe that right now, do you feel beautiful?" She said no that she didn't believe it at all.

When we say an affirmation over and over just hoping that it is true we are lying to ourselves and we know it! Hoping is a projected thought – you are not experiencing it you are hoping to experience it and these are not the same. One exists in the future and one exists in the now. We can only feel things in the now so make certain your affirmation is both believable, positively stated and written as a 'now' statement such as I am and I have.

I asked this young woman if she felt she was loyal, kind, and compassionate and she agreed that she felt like she was all those things. These are the affirmations that will help her: I am kind, I am loyal, I am compassionate. They will be effective and create change because they are of a high vibration and she already believes them to be true. From there as she changes how she feels about herself she will eventually get to say, "I am beautiful," to herself and believe it.

Getting into the belief stage is vital as we tend to operate out of belief systems. Many have become so ingrained that we do not think them anymore we just become them, which is a good thing if the belief serves you in a positive way, not so much if it is outdated or erroneous.

It is here where knowing how to move energy is very helpful. When I go into someone's energy field this old thought pattern feels tangible to me in an energy sense, meaning it has density, form and substance.

I then ask that density to show me where or when it was created. I use my intuitive knowing to get details, and the client and I have a great conversation bringing as much awareness and new perspective to the experience as is needed to shift the feelings around it.

I then can assist them with the movement of the density by putting my awareness onto it and pretty much blast it with love, gratitude, acceptance and understanding.

Love and gratitude are the highest and most effective vibrations you can use for transformation purposes. When we find the reasons behind the experience then we thank the issue for bringing so much information and learning to our awareness, and then we ask it to transform into light because its purpose has been fulfilled. I then surround the person and the issue with my own very intentionally high vibrating energy field and this high vibration breaks it up and assists the client in the transformation. This is what I meant earlier about the steam and ice cube.

The extremely technical term I use for this process is 'rinsing the dishes' (I so wish there was a humorous statement font). What I really do is that I perceive the density with them as they move it, and then as needed I break it up into manageable pieces and then I make certain that I GIVE IT BACK. I can do this because I CAN'T CATCH YOUR ISSUES. The experience isn't mine so I do not hang onto it, I just affect it in a positive way like I would if I rinsed the dishes before I put them in the dishwasher.

I form no attachment nor do I have ANY judgement around them, I just assist in the moving of the energy. The complete transformation will be up to the person it belongs to because it is their issue, their lesson, their experience so how diligently they work to change it will bring about their result.

My experience is that if I 'rinse it off' they have a more successful result because it has been energetically altered from its original state, and no longer reacts the same in their body nor do they react to it the same way.

The next step is the culmination of the process and it is all about the breath. Breathing is vital to our survival. I once heard someone state, "Humans are so funny they think they are breathing but what they don't realize is that it is your Soul that is breathing." You don't choose to breathe or not breathe; your soul does. Have you ever tried holding your breath? Right!? Not as in control of that as you think are you.

What I like to call the *Conscious or Vertical Breath* is when you take a deep breath on purpose. Where that breath comes from and the intent you have in it are very important. Taking a conscious breath means, you are intending to bring in the new thought pattern and replace and expel the old one. This is inhaling in the new and exhaling the old, the intent is to inhale light, high vibrating energy and let go of the old dense energy you had in your bankers boxes.

The other important aspect is from where are you bringing the breath. A vertical breath is going to be more effective than a horizontal breath. A horizontal breath is when you are breathing in the energy that is all around you; the chaos, the upset, the experiential world, it is like drinking the dishwater and it feels restricted and shallow. A vertical breath is when you visualize taking breath from a vertical source – from the universe – imagine gazing up into the deep blue of the night sky, layers and layers of light and stars, this is a fresh new breath that comes from Source, it is like drinking water flowing from the tap, and it feels deep and expansive.

Right now treat your Self and take a deep,
conscious, vertical breath.

So the process is:

1. Identify where or how the issue is showing up in the physical body.
2. Find the probable cause in the book's (You Can Heal Your Body) chart.
3. Discuss, ponder, journal where and when those feelings were present in your experience; do whatever it takes to find clarity.
4. Look at them with a fresh new perspective and understanding.
5. Decide if you would like to continue experiencing those symptoms, I am guessing NOT!
6. Say, feel and adopt the new thought pattern as a belief.
7. Take a deep conscious vertical breath.

8. Do it every chance you get.
9. Help someone else with the process because that is when it really gets fun!

Now that you are listening to your body talking, it's going to get very chatty. Be kind with yourself during this process and remember it takes time and energy to move your Self through the stored emotions in all your bankers' boxes. It will be easier if you approach the process with joy and excitement rather than see it as work and drudgery. It's hard work to go through all those stored emotions, which is why you stored them in the first place – you didn't want to look at them. Now you are choosing to do so and that makes all the difference but it can get exhausting, so nurture yourself, be kind, gentle and cut yourself some slack; rest, read, laugh, play and live life as you deal with your shadows – you are worth it!

Now that you are tackling those physical and emotional symptoms, it is time to introduce you to the mob godfathers of the human experience guilt, worry and hate.

Chapter 8

Call a Plumber....
I've Got a Clog in my Energy Pipes

"I no longer want the pain of my past and the fear of my future to decide who I am being right now."
~ *Personal Journal Entry 2006*

Okay maybe not a plumber, but an energy worker would be awesome. Even though we are all having our own human experiences there are some common energy blocks that we all share. Guilt, worry and hate really are the godfathers of energy clogs. Each one of them slows down and restricts your energy flow to such a degree that they can consume your thoughts, time and energy leaving you little energy for anything else.

Guilt and worry are the main causes of stress and ill health in many people. They can suffer for years wracked with guilt over their past experiences and spend a great deal of time and energy worrying over their future ones. As an emotion, hate creates a strong bond of low vibration and is an extraordinary drain on your energy fields. Finding ways to alleviate these insidious emotions would singlehandedly change the health of any human being immediately.

To move through and release both guilt and worry we must first be aware that all healing occurs in the eternal moment of now. Neither guilt nor worry truly exist in the now moment. So how do we heal things that have happened in our past or affect our future in a productive way?

Remember that emotions can only be felt in the moment of now. An emotion cannot be remembered or anticipated, only experienced. If you are thinking back to an incident in your past and the experience still makes you angry, sad or hurt then the incident does not exist in the past because you are still experiencing an emotion around it. Emotions exist in the moment of now because that is where we experience emotions. If you can feel it, you can heal it!

This is why we can heal things around our experiences because we still have an emotion around them. When we resolve the emotions around the incident and integrate the experience, we then disassociate from the feeling thereby healing the effects of that experience.

The reason it can be so hard to resolve guilt and worry is that they simply do not exist in the moment of NOW. Guilt and worry are more of a consequence of certain actions rather than emotions.

Guilt is something you have already done or not done; it is a consequence of a decision that you made in the past. You cannot change the experience at this point only resolve the emotions around it. If you are regretting the decision then you are feeling guilt around it, but the only way to alleviate the guilt would be to change the decision and you simply cannot do that because the decision was already made, the consequence was felt, and life carried on. You can make reparation or apologize but you cannot change the original decision.

Guilt is like trying to catch a fish <u>after</u> you have left the river.

Guilt cannot be resolved in the moment of now because it does not exist there and because we only truly live in the moment of now; this means that guilt is really an illusion and cannot exist. So this means we are constantly trying to resolve something that does not exist. This is of course impossible. We cannot resolve or heal something that is not there.

The same is true for worry. Worry is trying to solve problems that aren't here yet. It is trying to anticipate a scenario and prepare yourself for it. You are either going to have the experience or you aren't, you cannot prepare yourself for the feelings around it.

Worry is like trying to catch the fish <u>before</u> you get to the river.

If something disturbing occurs, you are going to have the emotions around it anyway whether or not you anticipated it or worried about before. You cannot truly prepare yourself for either pain or sadness. When something occurs that makes you sad or is painful, you are going to feel it even if you spent time worrying about the possibility beforehand.

You cannot 'bank' these emotions. When our youngest son was ten he said to me, "I'm worried that Grandpa is going to die." I replied, "One day Grandpa is going to die, he is in his eighties, and human life does come to an end and when that happens we are allowed to be as sad as we want. We are going to feel really sad when that happens and that will be okay because it is perfectly healthy and necessary to feel sad when someone we love dies, that is how we know we loved him because we are feeling sad. If we feel sad before he dies we are missing out on enjoying him while he is here with us and that is the most important thing we can do, enjoy people and things while they are here with us not worrying whether or not they will be taken away." Dad lived for six more years after that conversation and we enjoyed him while he was with us, and we were very sad when he passed, and we gave ourselves permission to be as sad as wanted to be.

Once again we are trying to resolve or deal with something that does not exist in the moment of now. Worrying or anticipating an event means we are in an illusion, the event or experience hasn't actually happened yet but we are expending our energy on the possibility of it and causing ourselves undue hardship. Trying to resolve an illusion is impossible as it doesn't exist, and it cannot be resolved, integrated or healed.

The fact remains that we do feel them and suffer from these emotions and we want to resolve them, so what do you DO about those pesky illusions called guilt and worry?

The best strategy for staying out of the illusion of guilt is to ask yourself, "Is there any action I can take right now that will help me resolve how I feel around this incident?" If there is, do it! If there is nothing you can do, then forgive yourself and move on and make a commitment to choose differently; the next time that situation appears remind yourself of this permission to just allow your Self to move on.

This quote by Neale Donald Walsch always assists me in dealing with the energy of guilt in a more productive way, *"You cannot change what happened, but you can change how you feel about what happened."*

This is the pure unadulterated truth because I know I can change my feelings; though I can't change what happened I can allow myself to shift how I feel about it, especially if I want a different result.

Both guilt and worry only exist in the brain, which buys into the illusion of linear time; your brain is the only place that the past and the future exist.

The effect worry has on your physical body is that your body responds to the worry as though it is actually happening. If you are worrying about someone being safe on the road and imagining all sorts of tragic scenarios, your body will respond to the thoughts as though they are really happening. What you think you are just imagining is really creating the same tension, feelings, and physical repercussions as though you were actually experiencing it in the physical reality. If it isn't happening where your feet are, it isn't happening. Keeping your thoughts, feelings and energy in this fiction called worry will become very detrimental to your physical health as time goes by.

One of the best strategies I have found around worry is to create a lighter energy especially in regards to the thoughts that are forming in my head. I will consciously stop myself from imagining negative outcomes and instead I will surround the person or situation with a pink light (this represents love to me) and I tell myself that no matter what happens I am strong enough to handle it.

I give myself permission to think about something else and thereby begin the process to re-train my brain to send positive energy rather than negative energy.

Once again, it is important to remember the ice cube analogy; if I am being density I create density, you can't throw mud at a mud puddle and get a smaller mud puddle. You have to apply a higher vibrational energy to affect density, so I can come in as water or steam to shift the energetic to a higher lighter vibration. Applying a higher more positive thought to the worry helps to minimise the energetic density in you and the energy that is being directed at them.

When we expend a lot of energy worrying about the state of other people we may feel like we are being useful and sympathetic, but what we are really doing is adding the same dense energy; you cannot create a higher vibration with dense energy. I must apply a higher, more positive energy to the situation or person if I want to affect it in a positive way.

I call this 'Thought Therapy'. If I am concerned about something one of my children is choosing and I start to think about it a lot and am worrying or rehashing an old argument or an old event, I replace it with a positive statement, "He is strong," or "We got this", or "All that is happening is happening perfectly."

I constantly allow myself to replace the thought when I catch it – sometimes I don't catch it so then I forgive myself and move on – and replace it the next time I become aware of it. I have found by doing this consistently; things seem to resolve much more quickly and I feel more emotionally detached and less invested, so then actual conversation and communication can take place rather than drama and traumas which are what worry and an overly emotional state creates.

Another common energy block or habit we humans get ourselves into can be seen in every media available to us, the expression of hate. Nothing ties you to someone or something more completely than the negative emotion of hate. Many events and experiences have been motivated by this emotion. Hate is a massive energy drain.

When you spend a lot of time, energy, and thought in the emotion of hate, you create a vacuum that sucks all of your energy away. You can react to hate in many ways by either avoiding or confronting this person or situation, but neither ever seems to relieve that pressure. This confrontation can be either physical or strictly mental. By mental I mean thinking incessantly about the situation or the events that have brought about the pain and distrust, confrontation or betrayal. All of this channels your energy into something that is not being resolved and ends up making you feel tired, cranky and depleted. If you expend your energy on the emotion of hate, it is YOU who experiences 'hurt' and then you cannot heal.

Why is this so? What does hate create?

Hate creates a barrier, a block that stops movement and when you stop energy from moving freely you create restriction and with restriction comes pain, both emotional and physical. When this block is in place resolution and healing cannot take place around the issue because healing requires a free flow of energy. Hate is a dense emotion, that is it vibrates at a slower and lower frequency than say love or joy.

To let go of something or someone you 'hate' you must do so with no negative attachments. Negative attachments create a bond of low vibration between you and the person or experience, and this is like an open wound constantly needing your care and attention. To truly let go and heal we must release the slower, heavier vibration and replace it with a higher, faster vibration like love, joy or acceptance. This isn't always easy, but it is necessary if you want to move forward from this experience and integrate and heal.

This happened to me in my teaching career. I had a principal who decided that he did not want me to be successful and used every means possible to make certain I did not have a job the next school year. He had fired me from my first full-time teaching position and this made me hate him for many years, yes years! I managed to get support from other professionals and remain in teaching but that experience haunted me. I ranted, raved, stewed, and hated him for many years. When I began my healing journey, I knew that one of the first things I needed to do was forgive and let go of this experience so that I could move on. In perfect cosmic timing, I saw him at a function and he didn't even know who I was!!!! Here I had carried this hate around for years and he was completely unaffected. The only person hurting and hating was me.

Healing can be achieved through forgiveness. I once heard somewhere that forgiveness is a gift we give ourselves, that we don't forgive for the other we forgive for the Self. That does not mean you condone or agree with their actions or opinions, nor do they have to play an active role in your life, but as long as hate exists inside you the more it consumes you and then they have power over you. I decided that I would choose to forgive him to free myself from the experience and how it made me feel.

I knew I really had to let this go so I worked through the processes I have shared with you using affirmations and redirected thought to help collapse those thoughts and feelings. I spent a few hours on this exercise and then decided to read a new fiction book I had bought to relax. I opened the book and the main character's name was the exact same as his – both first and last names. I started to laugh as here was cosmic validation of my process!

I had learned how and why forgiveness is so important; it is important for MY healing. It allows me to focus my attention on my journey and release the futility of trying to get reparation or satisfaction from a person who hurt me.

Neither of those things is possible. That person did what they did because of their own pain and anguish and I didn't really have anything to do with it in the first place. I was just the thing they took that pain out on; it was never about me, it was about them. I cannot heal what they are hurting from, only they can. Holding onto any negative dense emotion for them just hurts me further and perpetuates the pain.

It is to MY benefit to forgive them. They are in charge of their own pain, their own journey, and I do them a great service by no longer allowing them to hurt me because until I do that they are still trying to hurt someone in hopes that their pain will go away. Neale Donald Walsch says it perfectly; "*What has hurt you so bad, that you feel the need to hurt me to heal it?*"

If you can find it in your Self to step away from the pain and the ugly emotion called hate and forgive someone not for them, but for YOU, then you choose freedom. You are the only person that can heal you, you are the only person that can decide what hurts you, and you cannot heal anyone of their pain only they can.

Acknowledge that the people you feel hurt you are in pain themselves and until they turn and face their own pain, they cannot heal it and it is up to them to do that in their own way and in their own time. Give yourself permission to stop trying to change what they are feeling and feel the freedom this brings for you, lovingly leave them to heal their own pain, as you will do the same. Because you should love yourself enough not to allow others to hurt you in order to heal themselves.

Forgiveness is the beginning of your healing not an end...

These common energy drains are pivotal to your journey into healing and evolving your Self into peace, happiness and freedom.

The next thing we need to take into account when evolving into a more conscious creator of our lives is the art of MINDing your own business.

It's time to change your mind.

Chapter 9

Do You Have the Key to the Dressing Room? I'd Like to Change My Mind.

"If you want your life to settle down, to stop bringing you such a wide variety of experiences, there is a way to do that, simply stop changing your mind so often about who you are, and who you choose to be."

~ *Neale Donald Walsch,*
Conversations With God, Book 3

I have been on a personal journey of healing and evolving for many years and the single most challenging thing I have ever done is change my mind. It has taken the most time and energy for me to change the way I think about things and my beliefs around them. In an astrological sense, I do have many planets in air so I interface with the world around me in very intellectual way; with my noisy brain full of thoughts and the tendency to analyze everything it makes this even more of a challenging process for me.

I grew up on a farm and when you looked out into the pasture, you would find a variety of paths in the grass but there was usually one that was the main path to the barn. It was a very well defined path; the cows and horses had worn it so deep that grass would no longer grow there. It may not have been the shortest path to the barn but it was the one everything took because it was the most well travelled.

Deeply held thought patterns and beliefs are like that well-worn path to the barn. Changing your thoughts and beliefs can be like needing to leave that well-worn path and forge a new one. Your brain likes a comfortable well-worn thought pattern, it feels safe and secure when on it, it may not be the best thought or even a good one, but it is a comfortable one. This is your comfort zone.

As an energy healer, I find this the most difficult thing to affect in a client. I can help shift the energy in your emotional and spiritual-mind bodies but I cannot change your mind!!!! That is completely and absolutely up to you to do. You will need to think about what you are thinking about and see if the thought serves you in a positive or negative way. I can provide you with information, perspectives, and processes but I cannot change how you think or what you think that will be your responsibility.

I was substitute teaching in a Sixth Grade remedial class one day and a young man in that class said at least ten times in the first half hour, "OH! I am so stupid!" Finally, I said to him, "If you keep saying that you are going to believe it." He replied, "I do believe it." So my reply was, "What made you decide to choose the word stupid? What if instead of 'stupid' you said the word 'fast,' what would you be?" He looked at me very perplexed and answered, "Well I guess I would be fast." I replied, "Fast seems like a better thing to be than stupid but you get to decide."

I do not know what he did with my advice but I did see that for the first time he may have connected what he was saying with what he believed and that he was a part of that process. What I did observe was that he did not say he was stupid for the rest of our time together. That is what changing your mind is all about; becoming aware that what you allow yourself to say and think really does matter and it ultimately decides who you are and how you feel about yourself.

I often remind myself that if I have a certain thought a thousand times, what will I believe in the end? This helps me decide what thoughts I want to keep and which ones I am going to acknowledge and then just let go of them; if they don't serve a higher purpose or make me feel happy I just let them go.

Again and again I may have to acknowledge them and let them go because sometimes those thoughts are old well-worn paths that no longer serve me, so I will need to concentrate on making a new path until that path becomes the norm.

Many people have a very noisy brain; I am one of those people. I was a reluctant and often frustrated 'meditator' because trying to achieve a quiet brain without falling asleep seemed like an impossible task. I knew meditation was imperative to my growth and evolvement, as it is one of the few things that helps to fill up your energy reserves but I just could not achieve what I imagined a quiet meditative state to be.

I used guided meditations and they helped immensely to maintain and fill my energy reserves, but I usually fell asleep. I took a meditation class, learned some techniques, and had some good results but they were not consistent and I still found myself thinking. Finally, I realized that perhaps a quiet brain was not going to be my personal meditative state but I could achieve a focused one. So what I started to do in meditation was to focus my thoughts; I would only allow positive happy thoughts to stay as my brain chattered away. If the thought was not supportive or productive I acknowledged it, but then let it float away and brought my attention to a more positive thought.

This process really helped me to learn to monitor and choose what I was thinking about so that I did not allow negative self-talk, worry, projections or judgements to become the well-worn path. It wasn't easy, it was a struggle and when I started I needed to be vigilant because man my brain is stubborn!

The decision to focus only on positive thoughts brought about an interesting result; I lost the art of small talk. I began to notice that I had little to add to the social conversations I was in. I realized that a great deal of what people talk about in a social setting is negative and based in fear or competition. People just wanted to talk about it not go into the reasons around its creation or how we could ultimately change it, they just talked about the situation over and over with no thought to what that energy is creating.

I don't know who decided that the negative information you hear like the news, gossip and despair are reality and that positive conversation and seeing the bright side of things was 'rejecting reality', but I would like to give them a talking-to. I can't tell you how often I have heard people exclaim when I tell them I do not watch the news, read the newspaper or engage in gossip that they accuse me of living life with rose coloured glasses and that I don't live in reality.

My answer to that is, "You are right I don't live in YOUR reality, I live in mine. I like mine. How do you feel about yours? It makes you happy, healthy and optimistic does it?" I do not deny or reject that horrible, awful things are occurring in this world; what I am doing is not adding to the energy of them in my thoughts.

How does it help me to spend my energy thinking incessantly about these things? If I want to give energy to them then I best add an action to the thought. If I am worried about the starving children in the world, then it would serve me to get involved in changing that reality but sitting in my living room thinking about it, talking about to others and feeling bad helps no one; not them and certainly not me.

The truth of the matter is everything that you see around you started with a thought, even you. This is because:

Thought creates reality. All thoughts create reality.
Your thoughts about things create your reality.
What do you want your reality to be?
Choose your thoughts consciously.
If you don't like your reality, change your thoughts.

If we work from the premise that our thoughts are creating reality then we must be conscious of the thoughts we are sending and send them purposefully. This was illustrated perfectly by one of my clients who had a disagreeable and vindictive co-worker who she felt hated her, which created stress and unhappiness at work; she didn't want to quit her job but felt so bombarded that she was considering it. We decided upon a unique strategy for changing the situation. I asked her to place a glass of water on her desk and each time she had a negative thought (I call them *'thought bombs'*) about the co-worker, she was to see it going into the glass of water and dissolving. She was not to drink the water or give it to the plants, but at the end of each day she was to put it down the sink to be filtered, absorbed, and transformed by the earth.

She came to see me about a month later and said she had faithfully done this and was surprised by the result. Within a few weeks of doing this the co-worker stopped by her desk and said, she felt they hadn't had a chance to get to know one another so she invited her for lunch and they had a good chat; the negative feelings around her were absolutely gone.

The important thing to understand here is that the only thing that really changed was where the thoughts she was having were directed. When they went into the water, they were not going to the person she was stressing about and that simple redirection created a positive result. Why? I believe it is because our thoughts do affect the world and other people in the world even though they are not spoken aloud.

In fact I believe our unspoken, unexpressed thoughts are the loudest ones we have, creating all sorts of mischief for ourselves and others because if you were able to express them you would, and if you are not able to there must be a reason they need to be trapped inside you poisoning both you and the person they are directed at. You are going to be affected by your thoughts depending on what they are and so are the people you are thinking about. You will also be affected on some level by the thoughts that are being directed at you by others.

I often ask clients to consciously choose the thoughts they are having about someone (*thought therapy*); if you are worried or concerned about someone, sending them worried thoughts is not going to help. If you want to change the reality then you must send a higher vibrating thought to get a positive result. Also, remember that you may not get the result you want but at least you did not add to their pain or create pain for yourself. When you choose a higher thought it will inevitably change the result and assist you in changing your thought patterns.

This brings me to some of the thought patterns I had to change to create my reality, and one of the things I tackled and changed was the stories I told myself in my brain.

My mom and I drove out to my aunt and uncle's fiftieth wedding anniversary, and on the way there we passed the race track and I noticed that it was race day. On our way home, we were driving by the race track again and a police car had pulled someone over on the side of the road. I turned to Mom and said, "Oh someone had too much conditioning at the race track and looks like they got caught for speeding." Mom replied, "Well that's a good story." I was stunned! I realized that nothing about what I said was the truth but rather a fabrication based on random facts and observations. The only thing true about it was that there was a police car and another car on the side of the road. From that day on, I started to pay close attention to the stories I told myself – and found out I told them to myself ALL THE TIME! This wouldn't be so bad but I ALSO BELIEVED THEM!

I might as well have started all my thoughts with; "Once upon a time in a kingdom far, far away..." at least then I would be able to tell whether what I am thinking is reality or fiction. I came to realize that 90% of what I am thinking about at any given moment isn't actually happening; I am lost in a story from my past or creating one about the future. I am rarely in the moment of now, or *"where my feet are"*. My feet are always in the moment of now, but my mind rarely is. This normally wouldn't be so bad, but when I am focusing my attention on experiences or creating a scenario around future ones I cannot be fully in the most important moment - the one I am already in.

When we are replaying an experience or event in our heads over and over, we are reliving it by telling ourselves the story and as it continues to be our focus; we subsequently feel like the story never ends so resolution or our 'happily ever after' never seems to be achieved.

Something can happen in reality once but because we have mentally relived it countless times, it feels like it has happened more often than it actually has. Even though you are only thinking about it, the physical body responds as though it is happening in this moment, so it reacts accordingly, causing negative emotions such as anger, resentment, and physical tension because it feels like it keeps happening over and over again. If the thought stays constantly on the mind, even chronic physical conditions can be created. We can become so lost in stories from the past that they define who we are, and they move from something that happened to us to being an experience that decided who we are and how we view the world.

In his book *"Happier Than God"*, Neale Donald Walsch writes:

> *Decide that you are not your story. Our stories are made up of incidents large and small, spread out across a lifetime. We become the sum total of these encounters - unless we do not. At some point we may let go of an idea that we hold about ourselves and others, because we realize we have to if we wish to get on with life. Happiness will never be found in your story, only in your newest and grandest version about yourself and others.*

This may mean having to tell yourself, with regard to a lot of things that have occurred, "That was 'then' and this is 'now.'" None of those things have any bearing on what is occurring in this moment.

I decided to consciously avoid getting lost in my past stories and what an eye opening experience this has been for me. I realized first of all that I often recreate the story simply for my own entertainment, or to try bring myself solace, or even to justify something or feel powerful by replaying an event and imagining myself saying what I would have liked to have said when it actually happened.

Sometimes the stories are worst-case scenarios or speculations on what others were thinking or saying, but ALL of them are imaginary because they aren't actually happening. When we consciously decide not to give any energy to these stories, we free ourselves from unnecessary pain and suffering. By allowing ourselves to exist in the moment and free our minds to learn and observe we experience a sense of peace that was impossible to achieve when the mind was so busy with the stories it was creating.

So when you allow yourself to "let go of the story" and simply be in your physical world – experiencing and observing your life and the people in it - unadulterated by those 'Once Upon A Time' stories in your head, you have the ability to choose your thoughts and subsequently your reality.

This doesn't mean you can't think about your past; on the contrary I have found that impossible, I am learning so much from my experiences that I would not seek to forget them. What I am doing is thinking about them from where I am now after the fact and how much I learned in that experience, and using them as a way to evolve my understanding of my Self and others, not just replaying them like movies in my head.

I wish being trapped in our past stories were the end of our storytelling abilities but we also tend to do another type of storytelling which is 'projection', or the art of making stuff up.

This refers to the time when you are worrying about what might happen and how you are going to deal with it or what your reaction will be. I define worry as "trying to solve problems that aren't here yet." This is projecting your thoughts into the future, which isn't necessarily a bad thing when you are making plans and goals; that is not often what we are doing. Instead, we are dreading a situation or event and have started to create stories around what may or may not happen. We cannot truly 'prepare' ourselves for emotional upheaval, confrontation or distress as we will experience it regardless of our careful preparation.

This awareness allows us to stay in the present moment and not try to anticipate the event. When we think about it and try to solve it before it takes place, the emotional pain and suffering will then be experienced in the present moment. Your brain is a master of this. It can create any emotion at any time with a thought, and you will react to it because you are used to listening to your brain. In her book *"My Stroke of Insight"*, Jill Bolte Taylor (who suffered a stroke that shut down the left side of her brain), identifies her brain's creative abilities:

> One of the most prominent characteristics of our left-brain is its ability to weave stories. This storyteller portion of our left mind's language center is specifically

designed to make sense of the world outside us, based upon minimal amounts of information. It functions by taking whatever details it has to work with, and then weaves them together in the form of a story. Most impressively our left brain is brilliant in its ability to make stuff up, and fill in the blanks when there are gaps in its factual data. In addition, during its process of generating a story line, our left mind is quite the genius in its ability to manufacture alternative scenarios.... For the longest time I found these antics of my story-teller to be rather comical. At least until I realized that my left mind full-heartedly expected the rest of my brain to believe the stories it was making up! ....I need to remember however, that there are enormous gaps between what I know and what I think I know. I learned I need to be very wary of my storyteller's potential for stirring up trauma and drama.

We tend to believe the stories that our brains tell us because it is our means with which to make sense of the outside world, and to sort through all the data and remember things and how we feel about them. It's necessary that our brain learns from our experiences, but sometimes it does it when it's not necessary, and to our detriment.

This became very clear to me when I was working with a client on a strategy for shifting confrontation to conversation in her home environment. As we talked about the tool she could use to change this reality in her home, all of a sudden she was moaning and holding her head, very upset. I asked, "What happened?" and she moaned, "I can't do it!" I inquired, "How do you know?" She replied, "I thought about doing it at home and it didn't work!" I said,

"Well I have been here the whole time and you didn't leave, so that is not a reality". In that moment she found out how powerful her brain was. It could make her believe in five seconds or less that she would fail at her endeavour and she never left the room!!!!!

This is how we undermine ourselves and go into fear and suffering, because we believe we cannot achieve or handle the things that haven't happened yet. We haven't given ourselves the opportunity to truly experience something without mentally preparing ourselves for what we think will happen. If you can let go of those projections and instead identify when you are projecting, then you'll be aware that you really are just telling yourself yet another story.

As I stated in an earlier chapter, and bears repeating in this one, you have NO control over the thoughts coming into your head, but you do have 100% control over what stays. It is just that few people exercise the right to choose their thoughts instead feeling like the victim of them. You truly can be more focused and selective in your thought process and with this decision, you can create a far more conscious state of being through thought.

Deliberately and consciously changing your mind and tackling your thought patterns is one of the most amazing processes you will take yourself through on your journey to the Self. It is a freedom from the mind chatter and stress that will create peace and joy and allow you to participate fully in your life instead of surviving it. I mean you came here to thrive right? What kind of life do you want to create?

Chapter 10
So I'm Creating My Life....Now What?

"As the awareness of being the Universal Energy becomes your reality less and less will feel separate, even your feelings and messages. They feel as much a part of you as your arm, and the skin on your arm, and the mole on the skin of your arm. Everything melds together and makes your arm your arm. Nothing feels truly separate on your arm. It is the same when you integrate with the Universal Energy it feels like an integral part of what you already are. You are not 'discovering' it so now you can acquire it; you are merely 'uncovering' what has been there all along."

~ Channelled personal journey entry 2012

The process that I have brought to you up to this point has been the 'recognizing' of the things you are holding in your energy field, and the integration or releasing of the emotions and beliefs that created and maintained them. When we 'clean out' our store house of dense energy and start to operate from a lighter higher vibratory state, most people think "Wahoo my job here is done – everything is going to go great I am going to be an enlightened being who floats through life on a rainbow cloud throwing out the pearls of wisdom I have learned on my journey and I will be constantly peaceful and blissful and nothing bad will ever happen again".

Sorry to burst that delightful bubble, but that is just not the human experience.

Yes you will feel better than you ever have because things in your past are not weighing you down; you will have moved past the part of being human called 'reaction' and now you are far more conscious and deliberate – you have evolved on purpose.

So you may be saying, "What the heck Tanis! I did all that work and I still don't get to relax and manifest everything I want? What in the world did I do this for?"

This reminds me of a great quote I heard attributed to Buddha and it has been my reality check throughout my whole spiritual journey to evolve into a creative being. He said, *"Before I was enlightened I fetched wood and carried water. After I was enlightened I fetched wood and carried water, but I was happy."*

Yes, you do get to manifest and relax, just not in the way that you might have pictured it; you are not on vacation getting away from it all, you are in creation... creating it all.

What I am saying here is that you are not on a spiritual journey to stop anything bad from happening in your world. What I am saying is that instead of reacting and feeling powerless in the things that are happening around you, choose to use these tools and understandings to decide consciously who *you* are in the experience.

It is about choosing how you feel and how you respond to the things that are happening right now; that is the true meaning of evolving, getting out of reaction and into creation: to BE a creative Being rather than a reactive Doing.

So how do you shift from reaction to creation? Well clearing out and dealing with all that detritus in your energy field was the first best step. Now we can go into the tools you will need "create your life".

This is where we will revisit the all-important catalyst that I spoke of in the first chapter. Life will provide you perfect opportunities to consciously decide who you are. Whatever you decide to be will always create your result.

Pain is a good catalyst or motivator – probably one of the best and most useful in the human experience. People react to pain and seek to do something about it; in other words people do not ignore emotional and physical pain for very long without taking an action to stop it.

Many people embark on a healing journey because they are experiencing their own emotional, mental, spiritual and physical pain and are now motivated to change at a fundamental level for no better reason than to affect the pain.

I remember a time in my life when I used to ask the universe to please let me experience a day without pain. I don't want to say that my pain was any less or more than anyone else's, as I certain someone could trump my pain story with their own, but pain is pain and it doesn't matter the degree of it. Pain is felt intensely by everyone. Comparing your pain to someone else's is a good way to devalue your own pain and simply not deal with it. Ignoring or minimizing your pain means disregarding your own experience. You are having pain for a reason so don't dismiss it – use it to decide and choose something else.

It's like telling your child to eat their supper because there are starving kids in Africa; this is hard to relate to in your own reality when you are a child. I said that to my son once and he started packing up his food. When I asked him what he was doing he said, "Sending my food to Africa they sound like they need it." Make what you are experiencing real and relevant to what YOU are experiencing and stop comparing it to another's.

For a long time I couldn't imagine having a day without chronic back pain. I didn't have many moments where my mind would be quiet and my thoughts would be positive, I was very involved in the drama of my life. I used to start each new year with the resolution that I would be more positive and let go of guilt and worry and that I would do all I could to be happy.

What that really meant was that I wasn't feeling any of those things, because you rarely ask for what you already have. Somewhere deep down I knew that my pain and discontent were an opportunity for me to truly feel and experience true and complete happiness, and I absolutely knew that I was not yet experiencing it fully. I wanted more than just existing day-to-day hoping for the best.

Through my personal spiritual journey of healing and teaching others to heal, I am happy to say that I have created just that – happiness, a comfortable feeling of approaching each day with anticipation and delight. Feeling an acceptance and a sense of calm that no matter what today brings I am going to use it, as another great opportunity to choose to BE something I know will eventually return me to that state of peace and happiness.

It wasn't necessarily an easy adjustment, as it takes time and work and it is never really over, but the payoff is immense. The payoff is that you no longer live in your past or in your future but rather spend much more time in the present and that makes all the difference. As I stated earlier life is going to happen and what I want you to be able to do is to choose whom you are being **when** it is happening. I want you to be able to live from your center, from your intuition rather than from your busy noisy brain.

The questions remain: "How do you live in your intuition? What does that mean or look like?"

Living by intuition is giving the why's and how's of your life to the universe and choosing what you feel is right for you in the moment and observing and interacting with the journey, not trying to direct it or make things "right". Everything that happens to ourselves or someone is part of their journey and living by intuition means honouring that. It means you come from that loving place where there is no judgement or blame for the self or for others, just an opportunity to grow and change if need be. Intuition is letting go of control and being in the moment no matter what that moment brings.

I think you have three choices when you come to a conscious knowing that what you are experiencing is no longer serving you in a positive way. It is always best to choose the result you want, as this makes the choice easier. (psst, choose the third one.)

The first choice is to do what you are doing and get what you are getting; maybe not the best idea but it is a choice and a whole lot of people choose this one.

The second is to bail, to leave what it is you are doing and start again in a new place. That could be a new job, partner, or even a town, whatever it is you are seeking to leave behind you. This may look like a good choice but it is often temporary; you were part of the old creation, in fact you are the common denominator in all of your experiences, and if you do not make some fundamental changes you will create it again. Soon you will be experiencing the same results so this is often not a long-term solution.

The third is to change who you are in the experience. To consciously decide how you are going to interact with the situation in a way that supports you. Don't try to change anything external to you, but rather change how you interact with it so that you feel good about being in it at the end of the day. When you stop trying to change the experience and instead choose to change who you are in it, the only thing left to change is the experience itself. This is a good choice and it often creates magical results.

The truth is you have little or no control over the external world but you do have 100% control over the internal one. Stop trying to affect your internal reality by attempting to change the external world; it is a futile and frustrating endeavour. My good friend Ruby once said to me, "The position of manager of the universe is taken, stop trying to do that job." It made me laugh and still does, but more importantly it reminds me that I am not in charge of how the world is run but I can be in charge of who I am in it.

How do you do this? How do you become manager of your own personal universe?

I have already described the basics of personal energy but to refresh your understanding we are all energy and everything we perceive is energy. All tangible things are made out of molecules, and molecules have pure energy at their centers and this means that there is no empty space, that everything is connected.

This means that all energy has the ability to affect other energy even though we perceive we are separate from each other. This is why we can do energy work with each other. This is how 'psychic' works because sensitive people can perceive your energy body and 'read' it or interpret what they are seeing, hearing, or feeling when they are accessing your energy. Remember this statement as it is vital to understanding energy:

There is no such thing as empty space.

Energy is interacting with other energy all the time. All people are aware of energy all the time but they are not always 'conscious' of it. What I mean by that is everyone perceives things through their sixth sense but not everyone brings what they are reading into their conscious or aware mind. Some of us have chosen to build up and flex that muscle or hone that awareness and tap into it more often or more effectively than others; we are called psychic, intuitive, or weird! I love being called weird – if you look it up in the dictionary, the definition will surprise you.

We all have this capability, it is just more present in some than others. You have it and you are probably more aware of it than many others are. I know this because you are reading this book and have done all the previous exercises, so you are much more in tune with your energy being than you were before.

Ask yourself, "What energy am I being right now?" This simple question is the keystone between reaction and creation; these are the magic words that will change your world. This awareness will put you in the driver's seat of your own internal reality. Then if you consciously choose the energy you want to BE in that present moment you will create your result...every...single...time.

You already do this but you have been doing it asleep, like a sleepwalker, as a victim of what you are feeling not a creator of what you are being.

Four things are vital to the awareness and maintenance of your personal creative energy field.

The first of these is to *react*. To react is to strike back from a place of pain, previous experiences, or personal defence and protection. You are striving to defend and protect the Self and have emotionally engaged in the words or action. I always say to my clients when someone attacks your castle you automatically do two things, you defend and protect it. This is true when you are experiencing a real or perceived threat in all emotional situations as well.

To *respond* is the second, this is when we come from a place of power, understanding and knowing that the person cannot "make" you feel a specific way, nor are you bringing forward any unresolved experiences from the past. You are fully in the moment and observing what they have said or did and are not taking it personally. You are mostly detached from it on an emotional level; you are in fact (grab the popcorn) just watching it like a movie.

What does this look like in real life? Well imagine that all your life you have been scared of dogs and you are walking and a dog appears on the path in front of you. A reaction would be for you to go right into fear and run away (not the best idea dogs like to chase prey) or freak out and go into panic, that would be a great reaction!

A response would be to assess the situation from your experience because it has taught you that a dog who is making certain sounds or actions is one you must be mindful of and treat with caution. If it is sitting in the path in front of you with its tongue hanging out ready to give you a sniff and has a non-threatening stance, you are probably good to go. This is when you are staying in the moment and using your experiences to make a choice rather than just reacting to them.

When you choose to respond rather than react you have gained an immense amount of personal freedom and you will find that you are no longer subject to fear, bullies or manipulation because you are viewing the situation from a more powerful personal place. You are able to create a better outcome for everyone involved especially you.

The final two are about bringing personal integrity and authenticity to your experiences.

Personal authenticity is when what you are feeling and what you are saying match. This is when you eliminate the two conversations you are always having, the one from your mouth and the one in your head. When you are thinking one thing but saying another to someone, they can sense the disconnect and what they often perceive or conclude is that you are lying to them. You may be speaking a truth but if your energy and your words do not match, they will feel it and draw many erroneous conclusions from this disconnect.

Say what you mean and mean what you say; start matching what you are saying and what you are thinking. Allow yourself to be truthful and respectful. My advice in these circumstances is usually either say something or say nothing but accept whatever you decide to do and then LET IT GO.

Authenticity isn't always presented to you in a kind and gentle way; someone who is angry and yelling at you is being authentic in that moment. What we want is 'conscious authenticity'. As with 'responding' you know that how you are presenting yourself in the moment is going to get you a positive result, or at least one that does not cause you to feel disempowered.

Personal integrity is checking into what your own wishes and desires are in the moment you are presented with a choice and going with what feels right for YOU. Not what is socially expected or choosing what you think will make the other person feel better, or doing it out of obligation and 'shoulding' on yourself.

Instead you begin choosing for the Self, honouring what you truly feel like choosing. Not choosing to be selfish but rather Self-first and to be integral with what you know is best for you in any situation via your intuitive knowing.

Choose what makes you feel good about YOU and then you are honouring yourself rather than seeking something for the other person. Many think that this will make them egotistical and vain, but do you really think you would feel good about yourself if you deliberately hurt another?

Very few people who are sensitive to energy find hurting someone else satisfying but rather very difficult indeed. So often when we deny ourselves the feeling of joy to give it to another the only result will eventually be resentment and anger, and the sad part of that is you will blame the other when all along you were choosing them instead of you and that made you feel that way; they had nothing to do with it.

I have allowed my Self to experience staying in my personal integrity and authenticity, and when added with a dash of kindness and humility I have found that I never have been rejected for this. Instead of feeling resentful of my duties, I find that I am quite willing to do more than I would have when I did things out of obligation, guilt, worry, or the need for approval. I am no longer fixated on pleasing people and subsequently I can assist them from a place of joy and divine service and feel much happier than I did before.

As you move into a more creative way of living you will not only continually clear those pesky ice cubes from your energy pool, but you won't be making so many of them either.

As your energy field clears and strengthens you will begin to notice that your intuitive abilities will become heightened and more refined. We all have these psychic abilities and like any muscle, they need to be developed and maintained. Naturally as the ice cubes are melted in your energy field you will have less interruption or distortion and the flow of life becomes more effortless.

This begs the question of how will you know if you have truly melted those ice cubes? Well the answer may surprise you because you will find that life is really a great big circle and we are all just doing the Hokey Pokey!

Chapter 11

You Do the Hokey Pokey and You Turn Your Self Around, That's What It's All About

"Once you start 'being' a thing, you've engaged the gears of the most powerful creation machine in the universe – your Divine Self. Whatever you are being, you are creating. The circle is complete, and you will create more and more of that in your life. It will be made manifest in your physical experience. This is the greatest secret of life."

~ Neale Donald Walsch,
Conversations With God, Book 3

Have you ever heard someone say, "Why does this keep happening again and again to me?" They lament that they always get the short end of the stick and wonder why they can't succeed, be abundant, well liked, happy, content or a host of other things we all strive to be, do or have. Like the popular children's dance the Hokey Pokey, they feel like they are always putting things in but rarely getting much out of the experience just going around and around.

This type of experience is also something Steve Rother of Lightworker.com called "Circular Time". This concept demonstrates to us that as we move through our experiences we have a 'looping mechanism' built right into our timeline. Whatever we need to get out of the experience will come back around and around in the form of several events until we extract and learn all that it is needed for our advancement from similar experiences. These loops are not meant to be so annoying or to truly stop you, what they are for is allowing you to choose that third choice I spoke of in a previous chapter, and have continuing opportunities to change who we are in the experience and subsequently achieve a new result.

If we take the time to examine the details of the experience, the feelings and the result of the experience as a process of Self reflection, we will find the common denominator in each story and this can lead us to finding the sponsoring thought or the root of where in our timeline that it was created and continues to be created.

Each experience will have a similar thread that connects them all, usually a feeling, idea, truth or a belief that no longer serves who you are now.

When we identify those aspects we have the opportunity to change the energy around it, by choosing a new thought, word, truth, idea or a different way to be we then stop the creation of it or at the very least take a ninety degree turn and find a new path effectively stopping the looping effect.

Once you have reconciled or realized the personal reason for the experiences, and used the tools I have shared with you it will become fully integrated so that theme will no longer occur in your experience.

So be aware and watch carefully for the loops in your life because this is when you are having the experience of Circular Time. This is the part of the song where you get to change the meaning of 'you turn yourself around' because you will be consciously changing what you are experiencing from then on.

This loopy reality was illustrated to me very clearly in my own timeline. When I decided to leave teaching in a traditional school setting and become a full time healer, believe it or not I encountered a few skeptics along the way – shocking right?

These people sat in my office with arms crossed and demanded I prove to them that I was psychic, or that I had better help them or they would never believe in this stuff.

I remember being overly concerned and trying very hard to accommodate and bring them the experience they were demanding. Of course, this did not serve them or me in the long run so very soon I realized that their resistance and disbelief was a reflection of my own uncertainty about leaving a perfectly comfortable stable life as a teacher and embarking on a very risky, ground breaking personal path.

At this point, healers were not thick on the ground. Neale Donald Walsch, Deepak Chopra, and Wayne Dyer were making waves south of the border, but this was not an accepted practice in my neck of the woods.

I didn't want either my Self or my clients to be subject to this kind of experience. I wanted to be confident and accepting of my choices and beliefs regardless of someone else's opinion. I was like this in my teaching career as no one wants or needs a timid teacher in charge of their kids. To inspire confidence you must operate out of confidence.

One sunny day as I was sitting in my healing room looking out the window and pondering the process, I came to a decision. I decided that I am no longer going to protect or defend what I believe to be the truth. I am going to decide my beliefs and then just have them. I do not require that anyone else needs to believe them. I decided to no longer feel the need to explain my beliefs, or even what I do or how I can help them. Even if I am the only one who believes in me that is enough; the only one who truly needs to believe in me is ME!

I gave my Self permission to wait until they asked me for clarification or an explanation. My mandate from that point on that they must come to me already having the belief, or at least the curiosity and openness to agree that on some level this will benefit them in some way. I knew on every level that they are responsible for their own experience, just as I am. I am not healing them nor solving their problems for them, they are.

What freedom I experienced from this realization! What an incredible sense of Self I created when I decided to let go of the idea that I needed outside approval and support to do what I wanted to do and to be who I wanted to be.

This had an amazing side effect. I rarely if ever encountered another skeptic or non-believer and if I did, my internal feelings and the result of that opinion were so completely different that I did not react the same way. In many cases, I found that I didn't even realize that they had an opposing or fearful opinion. It would come to my attention only if someone else pointed it out or they made a point of telling me; I was completely oblivious because their opinion no longer mattered so much to me.

The result that I experienced as I moved this out of my 'need-to-prove-myself' belief system was that I no longer had that circular experience, that loop, where skeptics showed up to help me solidify and accept my beliefs. The reality of circular time is that you will be given what you are creating, so when I feared the judgement of skeptics and non-believers they showed up to demonstrate that fear to me. The reality is you need a catalyst to create the opportunity to feel this way and then change it.

You can't change how you feel if you are not feeling it in the first place. The experience is an opportunity to resist them and continue to feel persecuted or choose to change my belief and empower myself to believe in me. Just like the wound pokers I spoke of in an earlier chapter the universe is a giant copy machine; it sends you what you are being and the only answer it ever gives to you is 'yes'. So when I have the belief that people will not believe in me, the Universe sends people who don't believe in me and then says, "Yes that is true, look here they are, here are your hundred copies of that!"

As humans we tend to get caught in all sorts of perpetual loops that do not serve us in the long run. We tend to dance to the steps we were taught regardless if they match the music or not.

This brings me to another exceptionally useful creative living tool that has been of great use to me and that is to get your Self out of the Do-Do and into the Be-Be.

I was first introduced to this concept through Neale Donald Walsch's "Conversations with God" and it has become a deep and meaningful understanding that has assisted me in more ways than I can express.

Here is my reality of this concept: for eons humans have operated from a certain formula for their success, it is DO-HAVE-BE. People 'do' things so they can 'have' the things that will help them to 'be' happy, successful, abundant, etc.

What happened in actuality is that many people worked really, hard for many years at doing whatever they could to have the things they were seeking. What happened a lot of the time was that they became slaves to their 'doing' and this became the definition of who they are and many died from how hard they worked to get to the 'have' stage.

Those who got to the 'have' stage became very attached to their stuff and worked even harder to protect the things they achieved through their 'doing', always on guard that it would be taken from them in some way. Because some of the 'don't havers' felt the best way to 'have' it was to steal it from the 'doers.' That never makes the 'doers' very happy.

So if our wonderful 'doer-havers' manage to finally achieve the state of 'being' such as happy, successful and abundant, it was largely dependent on if they were able to keep their 'stuff' and if the stuff, status or title was taken away, they immediately had to abandon their hard-earned state of Being and go into DOing it again.

Whew! That is a LOT of work, time and energy being expended and you may not even actually achieve the state you want to be, and if you **do** you **have** to work hard not only to **be** it but to keep it as well.

From the standpoint of a creative being we can adjust the formula slightly to serve us in a more effective and efficient way. If we change the order of the words the formula then becomes BE-DO-HAVE.

We first choose a state of **BE**-ing that we would like to achieve like happy, successful, abundant, etc. Then we set out to **DO** the things that help us to feel that way. Once we have done that then we will **HAVE** that state of being.

In this process, you are less attached or concerned about your 'stuff' because you already have the feeling and that feeling is not attached to an external source like a person, thing, job or title.

When you put your feelings of happiness, safety, success, abundance or any of the other things that we are seeking to create into the hands of another person or object you will always run the risk of it being taken away. If you know that you are the one in charge of feeling and creating these things for your Self, then they cannot be taken away nor are they the responsibility of another.

Once you choose how you want to feel you can create it again and again from the feeling you are choosing to be. Now this sounds simple but we are very conditioned to DO and the old formula is utilized by so many more people than those who use the adjusted formula.

We have been conditioned for so long that our worth is directly tied to our ambition and assertive go-getter attitude. That life is a competition and if you sit on the sidelines, someone will beat you to the prize. No one tells you really what the prize is but everyone is chasing it. I am not convinced it is working, as when I look at the state of the world I see lots of people working hard but few are reaping the rewards.

If we look hard enough we will find those who are learning to stop racing to the finish line and instead are paying closer attention to the race. The collective is slowly changing but it is worth it to implement the BE-DO-HAVE formula in your life, because you will notice an immediate change in how you see and move through your experience.

This is an essential tool for moving out of reaction and into creation.

It's not about what you are getting out of the dance called the human experience it's all about what you are putting in!

You put your whole Self in.
You take your whole Self out.
You put your whole Self in and you shake it all about.
You do the Hokey Pokey and you turn yourself around.
That's what it's all about!

Chapter 12
Out Standing In Your Energy Field

"A man approached me at a trade show showing interest in my abilities so I asked if he would like me to demonstrate the energy work that I do as it is often easier to feel than to explain. There was very little energy exchanged when I placed my hands on his heart and so explained that this modality is not for everyone. He then told me of his disbelief in any of this 'stuff' that he had cured his cancer with raw food not any of this 'mumbo jumbo.' I listened intently to his story and when he finished I praised him for his strength and conviction to his healing. A few minutes later the vendor of the next booth came over and said he had stopped there and told her I was the best healer he had ever experienced. This taught me to recognize that you never truly know how energy will manifest and change the experience of another, just trust it!"

~ Personal experience 2010

This brings me to another modality that has served me well on my journey and has been felt by the thousands of people I have had the pleasure to assist; it is the power and wonder of hands on healing.

We all have the capability of doing energy work. We are all, always energy, we are all, always vibrating, and we are all able to manipulate and use the energy around us and in us with focused intention.

The energy in our body seeks to go into its original state of being which is perfect balance. When you are working with someone energetically you are seeking to help them to release denser energies; the only way this can happen is if you are vibrating higher than the person you are working with. That is why a healer's best and only requirement for helping facilitate a healing is to work on releasing your own self limiting beliefs and dense energies so as you become lighter and vibrate higher you will provide the vibration or space needed for the other person to heal themselves. All healing takes place at a higher vibration so maintaining your energy field and keeping your vibration high is vital especially if you are going to assist others. One of my favourite modalities in this area is "*Quantum Touch*" by Richard Gordon.

In Quantum Touch, you are using your vibration to facilitate the other person's release of dense energy that is stored in their body. That is why in a Quantum Touch session you are keeping your awareness mostly on yourself and where your vibration is rather than on the vibration of the other person.

"Everyone has the innate ability to help ourselves and others. The Quantum-Touch techniques teach us how to focus and amplify life-force energy (known as "chi" in Chinese and "prana" in Sanskrit) by combining various breathing and body awareness exercises. When you learn to direct the life-force energy, the possibilities are truly extraordinary; our love has more impact than we can

imagine. Everything vibrates. When two things vibrate at different frequencies, there is a tendency for the vibrations to come together. Most often, the slower vibration will rise to match the faster frequency.

Quantum-Touch uses resonance and entrainment to facilitate healing. The practitioner learns to raise his or her vibration and create a high level of energy. If that energy field is placed around an area of pain, stress, inflammation, or disease, that part of the body will entrain to the higher frequency and allow one's own biological intelligence to do whatever healing it deems necessary.

When the practitioner holds a high vibrational field of life-force energy around an affected area, she or he facilitates healing through the process of resonance and entrainment.

Richard Gordon, Quantum Touch

One of the reasons why I love Quantum Touch so much is that it begins with the premise that everyone can do it, that you do not need to be attuned to the energy nor does it need to be given to you by another. You are already an energy being therefore you have the ability to heal, vibrate and assist others with their vibration. I have also found that the speed and clarity of Quantum Touch makes it tangible to everyone. When I use Quantum Touch on someone, they always feel the effect it has on their body immediately, usually as a slight tingling sensation or their body begins to move on its own. Other healing modalities can be more subtle and less discernible for those less familiar with the sensation of energy healing.

When you consciously decide to use energy to heal with a focussed intention you are then capable of it – but you may not always be aware of what it feels like.

How to Feel Your Energy Field:

1. Rub your palms together in a circular motion.
2. Feel the generation of heat. This is your own energy.
3. Now hold your hands about two inches apart palm-to-palm.
4. Become aware of the slight pressure that exists between them.
5. Visualize your hands pushing toward one another.
6. Feel the resistance, similar to two magnets repelling each other.
7. Hold that feeling in your awareness, this is your energy field.
8. Begin moving your hands apart holding that feeling.
9. Establish the distance at which your palms can be separated and you still feel your energy. If you lose the feeling, bring your palms closer establish the feeling and pull slightly apart again.
10. With practice, you will be able to increase the distance as you become more sensitive to energy.
11. Another way to perceive the energy between the hands is to intentionally disrupt it, have someone pass their hand through your outstretched palms without touching your hands; you will feel a slight interruption in the flow, which of course proves there is a flow.

Once you get comfortable with holding the energy in your hands and body you can become a conduit for bringing Universal Energy through you and into the field of another seeking assistance.

1. Imagine all the energy of the universe circling above your head, available for your use.
2. Bring in energy through the top of your head or crown and collect it in your heart area.
3. Feel your intention to assist flow through you.
4. Send the energy from the heart area down through your arms, out your hands and into the person.
5. Imagine a complete circuit of energy flowing through you into the other out their feet back into the Universal Energy in a never-ending energy loop.

This a practical way to familiarize yourself with how the energy feels to you. If you can already feel the energy in your own way go with what you know to be true – your way of moving energy will always be perfect to you.

This brings up a concept from the old paradigm of healing that comes up as soon as I introduce energy therapy or hands on healing to others: the concept of 'protection.' I was taught to protect myself from the 'low' energies of others at the beginning of my Self-discovery and this made perfect sense to me until one day someone said to me, "Protection is a fear based concept not a love based concept." This simple sentence completely changed everything for me.

I do not approach healing or Self-empowerment from the energy of FEAR. I come at it from a place of LOVE. What was I afraid of? Your Energy? How could I protect my Self from my Self? Because from an energy standpoint there is no differentiation at this level there are only degrees of density and lightness.

We do need to protect the vulnerable physical body because it is fragile and vulnerable to attack and violation. It needs to be protected from external forces such as heat, cold, other people and physical abuse of any kind. Wear your seatbelt, use a helmet, don't wander around in the park at two o'clock in the morning and get away from those who would hurt you in a physical sense because all of these things can damage the physical body.

The emotional, mental and spiritual bodies do not require the same kind of protection. Protection for these bodies comes from the inside and from the frequency they are vibrating at. You bring to you the things that match your vibration – this is the law of attraction or resonance in action. Remember my earlier comment about the universe being a giant copy machine; if you are vibrating at a level of fear and anxiety, you will find that your experiences will match that. You maintain and 'protect' your intangible bodies by keeping them at a high vibration.

I was once working with a young girl who was having trouble with a group of friends; they had separated and were no longer friends. I asked her if she had made any new friends since and she said she had. I then asked her if her new friend was sad or depressed. She thought for a moment and said that yes she was and that this concerned her. I told her you brought this friend to you when you were in a sad state and she matches that state. She was astonished at the parallel and so we spoke about ways she could change that. I asked her to concentrate on a project for the next two weeks that brought her a lot of joy and passion. Then see what she creates in her life and how it helps both herself and the others around her.

I do not surround myself with white light, or protect my energy from other people's energy in any way. I do not believe that I will absorb any dense energy that you are carrying because I am not having your experiences I am having my own.

I can't catch your issues! To take on your issues means that they are my responsibility and they are not! It means that I somehow created your situation and am now having your experience of that creation, this is simply impossible.

Allow yourself to feel internally protected by your intuition and your internal knowing of what is right and wrong and know that these energies and your consciously created vibration are capable of 'protecting' you.

Though once again I would ask what in the world you are protecting your Self from, because energy is all around us all the time and we cannot be separated from it even if we tried. That is like peeing in one corner of the swimming pool thinking that if you are not in that corner you are not being exposed to the pee!

No one is truly allowed to access or affect your internal energy bodies without your permission - always know that you are in charge of these. Don't get me wrong, people can be really mean to other people and hurt them very much but again this is usually in a physical way. When we allow others to affect our feelings or self-worth, we are giving away our power to an external force or thing and that will never create a feeling of safety, security or protection. You are always in charge of how you feel even if it doesn't seem that way.

This does not address the sensitivity that many healers experience. Energy sensitive people can be adversely affected by the energy of others just through proximity. I spoke of this at length in the chapter about creating boundaries. In my own evolution I found that as I got a really good sense of my boundaries I could then get an upgraded filter system that requires little maintenance or thought.

I know that a high vibratory field helps create a vortex of energy that fundamentally protects you from being affected by the density around you. So it stood to reason that if I want a filter that assists me in this that I will need to create a vortex of high energy around my Self.

The most effective and efficient way to do this is to SPIN your energy field. Remember when I likened your energy field to a large pool of water? If you have a placid and quiet energy field all around you, you are more susceptible to the chaotic energies from the external world. The disruption and density that you are being exposed to will mix with your field and create chaos. This is how it can appear that you have absorbed someone else's energy problems or given them yours.

Imagine how a smooth quiet lake is affected when a bunch of rocks are thrown into it − it causes all sort of disruption that affects the whole surface of the lake. Now imagine throwing those same rocks into a whirlpool − the surface already has so much velocity that it directs those rocks down and out the bottom without too much disruption to the spin.

If you spin your energy field like a crazy tornado, you create a perfect movement to deflect external energies and spin them away while maintaining and sitting exclusively in your own energy field. Remember to stay in the eye of the tornado where it is still, as moving out into the spin can create vertigo-like symptoms that are very disruptive and alarming.

You have created a high vibrational energy field and it can even assist others in a positive way because your high-energy field is spinning at such a velocity that it encourages them to do the same through the same entrainment process we use in Quantum Touch.

This spin creates a perfect filter for you to be aware of the energy but not absorb the energy of others, this puts you into an observer state and this is where you can BE empathy, compassion and grace.

It is important to remember that energy attracts like energy, so when you are vibrating at a low, slow dense energy that same kind of energy will be attracted to you, this is the law of resonance or attraction.

Everything I have spoken to in this book is about transforming your dense energy into a higher lighter vibration. This automatically creates a higher vibration and so you cannot attract the same kind of dense energy to you that you did prior to your Self work. This is also an energetic form of 'protection' for your energy bodies.

I do not feel separate from the Universal Energy or anything in it and so I do not think that any energy has the potential to harm me; heal me yes, but harm me no. There is nothing outside of who I am in an energy sense. If I want to throw a pen away and put it in the garbage, well the garbage and I are in the same room so we have not been separated yet. The garbage man comes and takes it to the landfill, but I live in the same district, so nope still not separated. I get a rocket ship and I put the pen on it and send it up into the solar system, wait, I live in this solar system – so nope we are still not separated...do you see where I am going? There is no such thing as 'away'.

You are part of the energy, always have been, and always will be. You cannot get 'away' from it but you CAN decide who you are in it. Are you going to vibrate at the higher, faster level or the lower, slower level? It is up to you.

When you decide to BE part of that Universal Energy in a conscious way you have some amazing perks....and having access to divine guidance through your intuition is one of the best!

Chapter 13
When You're Write – You're Write

"I find I am resisting the word 'channel.' Why do I resist this concept? At first I just thought I couldn't do it because only really amazing people can truly channel or maybe it is because sometimes it feels like I am making this all up and just writing what I want to hear. Or maybe I am afraid I will write something I don't want to hear. After learning how to do it in a way that worked for me I had great success and what I did find in the process was that I am so much more connected to my Divinity than I could ever have imagined."

~ Personal Journal Entry 2012

I use a very helpful and necessary tool to assist me with the process of paying attention to what I am creating. I use a channel journal...I know, I know you will be all like "yuck! I hate journaling, I used to journal but now I just have gotten away from doing it." Right? Well I did too. Just journaling as a recitation of the current situation was tedious and something I never returned to read again because frankly my play-by-play is kind of boring even for me.

My good friend Ruby is an automatic writer and her insights and perspective are very valuable to me. One day after a reading she asked me why don't I do any automatic writing? I laughed, "That's your gift not mine." She said that automatic writing is just as much about being aware of and channelling your intuition as the empowerment process I am doing with people and my Self. She encouraged me to try it.

I wasn't very successful at first and tried many ways to journal my channel but kept being restricted by my very critical left-brain. I found that being a teacher for many years had settled me firmly into the left side of my brain when it came to writing. I would automatically go into judgement and evaluation of my writing rather than just allowing myself to write for the sheer joy of it.

When you can bypass that logical critical side you find that you are capable of insights and wisdom that go beyond what you 'think' you know and go into what you already know and understand at a universal level.

I tried many ways to get through that critic and allow my brain to channel the energy on demand rather than waiting for those occasional flashes of insight or only having them when I was working with a client.

When I speak of channel I mean that you are going into your higher Self to truly have a chat, not just writing what your left brain wants you to write but literally getting into the intuition which is housed in your right brain. It is that unstructured Essence part of your Self.

A new concept to approach the task was introduced to me by a dear friend Brenda. She is trained in hypnosis and she shared one of the techniques used in that modality called the "Confusion Technique". It worked perfectly for me to get past that teacher's left brain and into my Essence and now I would not be without this tool.

Here is how it works: you take a fresh clean piece of paper (preferably unlined) and you start to write down every word your brain is telling you, I mean every word! As random, weird, and ridiculous as they are, you will continue to write them until your mind has a temper tantrum, it will kick and scream and tell you this is stupid (write that down too) and just generally kick up a fuss. Allow yourself to stay with that and write as fast as you can for at least fifteen minutes. Do not allow yourself to stop until that time is up.

Then go back through and read it aloud to yourself and notice if any of the words have a resonance or a feeling to them; some may or may not just pay attention and circle them.

Do this again and again as often as you wish until your left brain throws its hands up in despair and allows the right brain to take over. You will begin to see more and more words circled or they will begin to form sentences and they will be words of encouragement, insight on your current situation, or even answers to the questions you have been asking yourself.

Getting yourself up to writing more than 400 words in fifteen minutes means that you have a better chance of shutting out the critical part of the left brain. When this happens you get into the live streaming information of the Universal Energy that is your intuitive Self.

Pay very close attention to how the words feel because messages from your higher Self, which is a much more expanded part of you, always feel momentous. I compare the feeling to the sound of a gong going through you or they can be accompanied by a tiny thrill or just a simple deep-down knowing that these words are different from your human voice. Soon you will not have to write the words that your left brain is saying because you will have trained yourself to go directly to the right brain. You are now channelling your higher Self and getting guidance from that all knowing Universal Energy.

My favourite way to utilize this skill is to ask my higher Self a question around a process or current situation and then channel the answer. As I write I find that I am fascinated and excited by the information that is coming through, which means of course I am not thinking these things otherwise I would already know the answer.

If the messages are critical or foreboding then recognize that you are not in your Higher Self but rather you are talking to your fear. Your Higher Self or your Soul does not reprimand or criticize it is pure love all the time so if the messages are not encouraging or helpful, then you are in your critical left brain or in your past conditioning so take a breath, write words until the left brain surrenders, and then go ahead and write again.

I have filled four journals in three years doing this and I am so grateful for the information in them as they are the reason that I was able to write this book. I knew how to have my left brain surrender and let my Self come through and write from a Universal Energy standpoint rather than just a recitation of my process with no feeling or energy attached to the words.

My favourite client story around this process is when I suggested this to someone I had known for a long time. I explained the process and as I asked her to give it a try, I could sense that she was very skeptical almost to the point of dismissing the process as silly and was wondering on the inside, "Did I just pay this crazy lady for a session?"

As she left I could tell she was very disappointed and uncertain about the validity of the suggestion so I called out to her as she walked away, "You are going to love me after you see what this will do!"

Several months later, I saw her again and she said, "You know I thought you were crazy, totally bonkers but I trust you so I tried it, and I started to get messages! They didn't sound like me and they were so helpful and encouraging that I have already filled a book and can't imagine myself not doing this every day. Thank you!"

I call this form of communication 'my guidance' because it is my Higher more expanded Self guiding me through my evolution and understanding. This channelling process brings me so much clarity and solace that I wanted to share the process with you so you can create this internal support system for your Self as well.

Not to mention that then you will literally be.....Talking to Your Self.

Chapter 14
Look Who's Talking

"I have never lost sight of the fact that my main focus is my own evolvement and expansion. That every minute of every day I am in the conscious creation of my Self and that being able to assist others to do the same is a beautiful side effect of that process."

~ Personal journal entry 2014

I have deliberately not referred to the title of this book or why it is called that until now. I wanted to set the stage for you to realize that there truly is only one of us, that we are one massive Universal Energy field and that there is nowhere you need to go to heal or empower your Self other than inside.

When you stop living from the outside in you shift your whole perception from reaction to creation.

You are the creator of your life.

On all levels, in all moments, you are in the active creation of your own life.

I have covered many concepts and strategies that will help you gain a deeper understanding of the Self, and you must have realized by now that we are indeed talking to ourselves.

That the only perception we have at any given moment is our own. No one else can see the world from where we are standing because we are the only one occupying that space. It is the knowing of this that sets you free to have your own experience rather than constantly having your attention fixed on the experiences of other people in your life.

It stands to reason that if knowledge is power then knowledge of the self must be self-empowerment. You are empowering the Self because you have discovered that your body is a great warning light and you have listened to those warnings and actively and on purpose melted your ice cubes. You found out that those pesky wound pokers are actually a blessing, you have your mind on track, focussed and purring along like a cat and you are now operating more from your internal knowing, respecting your boundaries and the boundaries of others and best of all learning to put yourself first.

When these things are made part of your conscious life you feel more centered and better able to navigate the world you are currently in; not trying to create a new one but truly be present in the one you are standing in.

When you make Self your commitment you start to make peace with what is happening around you, which then translates into a new reality – not a new life situation but rather a new reality of the situation you are all ready in.

This is so vital and important to understand so take these words with you wherever you go:

"I am creating my own reality right now."

This is the creation process you are engaged in:

What you are being you are creating.
What you are creating you are bringing to you.
What you are bringing to you, you are experiencing.

If you decide that you don't like what you are experiencing you will need to change what you are being, not change where you are living, whom you are married to, trading your kids in or getting a better body – you literally need to change what you are being at a fundamental personal level.

Creation is a lot like making a cake; you put all the ingredients together in bowl, mix them all together and then put it in a pan, bake it and then cool it and finally you will get to take that first bite. The reality of this cake creation is that you cannot know what the cake tastes like until you bite it. This is just like your experiences, as you don't know what you are truly being or creating until you are experiencing what you have created.

You don't taste the cake and say, "Well yuck that tastes terrible I will never, ever make a cake again!" No, you adjust the ingredients or use a different recipe until you make a cake you like. Your life is the same – do not define yourself by the experiences you are having, use them to decide what parts of YOU you would like to adjust or tweak.

You can only do this in the current situation because this current situation is your creation and you get to decide who you are in it. You cannot affect the cake at the point that you are eating it. The creation process happened during the construction of the cake, so don't get so attached to your current situation that you cannot see the blessing in it. Watch for that Hokey Pokey process or Circular Time where you discover if you like the cake you baked for yourself. If not, go back to the internal ingredient level and adjust from there until you notice you are getting the results you want.

In the new paradigm, the governing or motivating force is not fear it is FAITH. Faith requires us to trust and know that everything is conspiring in our favour. It becomes less about where we are going and more about where we are; the present is where we are creating our life experience and our Self, not in the past or future.

When you place your focus and intent on the present moment where you 'ARE' then whatever you are BEING in the moment creates the next one and so on. So it becomes less about the journey and more about 'real-time creation'.

Like the workings of a Swiss watch, when all the components work perfectly together it is impossible to remove one part and have the watch still work smoothly. The universe is like that; it is all working together to create in perfect harmony and synchronicity to simultaneously create your known reality. Every part is doing its part perfectly and we are an integral part of that system.

It is the illusion of control over the external world that separates us from the Whole; you have control over how you show up in the Whole but not over the Whole. You are an intricate and necessary part of the Whole but the only part of it you can truly affect is YOURS. This is a paradox because you have ultimate control and no control ....

"It is arrogant beyond measure for you to believe that you can affect the universe in a way with which the universe does not agree. You are dealing with mighty forces here, and some of you believe that you are mightier than the mightiest force. Yet you are not. Nor are you less mighty than the mightiest force. You ARE the mightiest force. No More, No Less."

Neale Donald Walsch, Conversations with God

When you have expanded your understanding, of how you fit into the Whole, then you have crossed that line from feeling separate from others to knowing you are not and this changes immediately how you perceive them. The further into the unified energy field you go, the less separated you feel from everything.

In our old separated paradigm that operated from fear, we felt that "Everyone is out to get me." In the new unified paradigm, we operate from the all-inclusive energy of "Everyone IS me."

This is not something you really need to learn to do as it is already happening; it is something you learn to be comfortable with because it is a by-product of your more aware state of being.

We never develop these gifts or sensitivities for no reason. Your interest in the Holistic field or healing your Self is not random or by accident: you are meant to contribute in some way, you already are, you always have been, and now you are asking to be more aware of what it is you are contributing, and that is all you need to continue to do.

There is nothing specific that you have to DO. It all comes down to what you choose to BE and from there all is created and experienced. A state of being is something you can do no matter where you are or what you are doing.

It is all about the BE!

I love to visualize that unified field of energy as all of us in our expanded, all knowing state, sitting in a coffee shop as a cosmic coffee circle helping each other by sending messages down through the experiences and interactions of our human selves. We get the messages we need to find our way through the amazing experiences from each other as we create in the

151

illusion of being separate from each other and ourselves. In truth we are one massive energy field divided up into amazing individual pieces that work simultaneously and symbiotically to create a whole experience so that we might know ourselves.

So this message is from my Higher Self coffee circle buddy to yours:

Thank you for gifting yourself with this book and this process. It is my intention for this book to have been a catalyst for you to evolve on purpose and get to know who you are on every level of being. To consciously decide how you would like to show up in your unique experience.

It is meant to help you transform and embrace the dense experiences you have had in your life and see them from a new perspective which frees you from the physical, emotional, spiritual and mental effects they were creating.

It is my intention to provide you with the means to help your Self because freedom from the struggle of trying to manage the external world and the people in it is a beautiful and peaceful thing to create. It is possible only if you go within, only if you get really good at Talking to Your Self.

Thank you for allowing me to assist you with your human experience.

This is my Personal Prayer and Mantra.
I invite you to experience it, share it
And in times of great stress and uncertainty
BE IT...

~

I am the Faith of Allow

I am the Power of Presence

I am the Stillness of Creation

~

About the Author

Tanis McRae B.Ed.

When asked, "What do you do?" Tanis always replies with, "Whatever it takes!" And it's true, She is fascinated by people's stories and dedicated to assisting them on their healing journey and her goal is to work her way through the 7 billion people on this planet until everyone creates their own personal feeling of happy.

She is an innovative practitioner of the healing arts, with 10 years of experience helping people to take charge of their personal health and wellbeing. She employs an effective self-designed process that enables people to release emotional blocks and transform the dense energy of pain and trauma into the ability to enjoy happier, well-balanced lives. This process includes a lot of laughing and moments of pure silliness. Her 20 years of experience as a teacher also enables her to communicate her message in a clear, easily understood manner to clients of all ages because when we start learning something we are all Grade Ones at heart. Her workshops and private sessions provide people with an opportunity to learn her methods of self-healing and evolvement creating independence and sustained results.

Tanis lives in Grande Prairie, Alberta, Canada with her husband and two grown sons.

Find out more at www.thehealingi.com